Also by Charlton Heston

THE ACTOR'S LIFE: JOURNALS 1956–1976

查尔顿·赫斯顿

一种虚荣,真正有价值的是自己的切实工作,这才是引以为荣的。"正是基于这种治艺思想,他一向刻苦勤奋,很少参加宴会和交际场合。同他在一起生活了 40 多年的林狄亚不无感慨地说:"作为他的妻子,我真希望他能减轻一些工作负担,让他享

好象是不太可能的。"

作为一位出色的艺术家,赫斯

他酷爱读书,经常欣赏音乐,观摩美

曾在纽约画廊举办过展览。多年来

1956 年至 1976 年的日记编辑出版

畅的文笔记述了他的艺术道路、创

的情况。成为深受读者喜爱的畅销

以演电影著称的赫斯顿也非常

演舞台剧同样重要。演电影拥有更多

表演技巧。"由他导演的话剧《昼行

录,由他主演的《一个适时的人》《

都广受观众的欢迎。1971 年,赫斯

东尼和克里奥佩特拉》搬上银幕,并

响。此外,一贯强调演员社会责任感

家。他曾六任美国电影演员协会主席、国家艺术委员会主席。1977 年美国电影与科学院授予他琼·赫谢尔特人道主义奖。现任美国电影学院院长。

BEIJING DIARY

Charlton Heston

Introduction,
Photographs, and Captions by
Lydia Clarke Heston

SIMON AND SCHUSTER
NEW YORK LONDON TORONTO SYDNEY TOKYO SINGAPORE

SIMON AND SCHUSTER

SIMON & SCHUSTER BUILDING

ROCKEFELLER CENTER

1230 AVENUE OF THE AMERICAS

NEW YORK, NEW YORK 10020

COPYRIGHT © 1990 BY AGAMEMNON FILMS

DESIGNED BY EVE METZ

A LEATHERBOUND SIGNED FIRST EDITION OF THIS BOOK HAS BEEN

PUBLISHED BY THE EASTON PRESS

MANUFACTURED IN THE UNITED STATES OF AMERICA

1   3   5   7   9   10   8   6   4   2

LIBRARY OF CONGRESS CATALOGING IN PUBLICATION DATA

HESTON, CHARLTON.

BEIJING DIARY: CHARLTON HESTON; INTRODUCTION,

PHOTOGRAPHS, AND CAPTIONS BY LYDIA CLARKE HESTON.

P.   CM.

1. HESTON, CHARLTON—DIARIES.   2. WOUK, HERMAN, 1915–

CAINE MUTINY COURT-MARTIAL.   3. WOUK, HERMAN, 1915–

—STAGE HISTORY.   4. PEKING (CHINA)—DESCRIPTION.   I. TITLE.

PN2287.H47A3   1990

791.43'028'092—DC20

[B]   90-41604

CIP

ISBN 0-671-68706-9

Grateful thanks are due the following:

Henry Holt and Company, Inc., and Brandt & Brandt Literary
Agents, Inc., for permission to quote from "American Names,"

(continued at back of book)

THIS BOOK IS DEDICATED TO HERMAN WOUK.
HIS PLAY HAS CHALLENGED ME, TAUGHT ME,
AND REWARDED ME AS BOTH DIRECTOR AND ACTOR
ON THREE DIFFERENT CONTINENTS.
I'M DEEPLY GRATEFUL.

BEIJING DIARY

INTRODUCTION
by Lydia Clarke Heston

Did our blood run faster at the thought of two months in Beijing? Of course! But with such different dreams, such varying apprehensions. Chuck was plunging into what seemed to me an impossible challenge: to transport an American play—granted, one he knew well both as actor and director in English versions—but using Chinese actors performing in their own inscrutable language, of which he knew not a word, to a Chinese audience. My own aspirations were more modest, but still daring: to absorb, digest, and understand that ancient culture, and to record what I saw with my cameras.

Chuck was enticed by what we used to call the "smell of greasepaint," an inspiration of some forty-five years in theatre and films. I was beguiled by a long association with two superb Chinese artists, Dong Kingman, whose bright and delicate watercolors grace our home, and Chin San Long, called the "Father of Chinese Photography." Dong is a New Yorker now, and Long (I must remember to use the last name first!)—if he is still with us at one hundred plus—was one of the brave Chinese who dared the dash to Taiwan.

How typically Chinese was Long's appearance at an exhibition of his subtle photographs that I held on our tennis court in 1978. I was so concerned about his aging health (86) that I had placed chairs at every corner. Long—tiny, pointed beard and twinkling eyes—arrived in his Mandarin costume. A heavy Hasselblad camera hung from his neck, and he never sat down once during the entire evening. How vigorous they are! As historian George Carrington remarked, the Chinese are *hearty!*

Both Dong and Long gave me a profound interest in the Chinese—their sensitivity, their fundamental loyalty to Chinese values and the thousands of years of Chinese culture that drew them both into the twentieth century.

Chuck and I had seen Taiwan and Hong Kong, had noted the strong work ethic invigorating both of those vital, romantic locations. How on earth, I wondered, could the incredibly enterprising mainland Chinese bind themselves, as they once bound the pitiful feet of their women, to a system so limiting, so debilitating, as Chinese communism? I couldn't wait to find out, feeling rather tense about what I'd discover.

My first days in Beijing I spent watching the rehearsals in the People's Art Theatre, apprehensive about how the performers would accept my presence. I needn't have concerned myself; smiling shyly, they plied me with cup after cup of dynamite tea. The two interpreters, speaking idiomatic English, were easily approached with questions about what to see and do.

Knowing Chuck would be glued to the play, we had asked a friend from Paris to fly in to explore the city with me. Meeting Maggie at the airport was a bit of a shock; it seemed that all one billion Chinese were meeting their friends, too, and of course there are no signs in English or any other language but Mandarin. I finally extricated myself from this impasse by guessing that a man wearing glasses might speak English. As is my habit when visiting where I don't know the language, I had learned a few phrases. Hesitantly I asked, "Ni shuo ying-wenma?" (Do you speak English?) I was more than relieved to hear a strong "Yes!" With the help of this dear man I found Maggie leaning on her walking stick near the unmarked Air France, and we were off in high spirits to embrace the Capital of the North: *Bei* (north), *jing* (capital).

"How wide the streets are!" exclaimed Maggie.

"They have to be for all those rush-hour bikes," I explained, as the bikers swung madly around us.

I had imagined a dark-gray, dingy city, with a populace dressed in similar clothes. What a misconception! Beijing is now full of greenery, and the people, particularly the children, sport bright-colored shirts above blue jeans or short skirts, often with misty-colored dust protectors covering their faces. Elderly women in white, also swathed in dust covers, swept the streets with an intensity that stunned us.

At least they did then. One of our first surprises was the openness with which many of our English-speaking friends discussed the government and their feeling that change must come. These conversations made me acutely uneasy, though I saw few overt signs of oppression. One small indication of military-mindedness: where our children would sport cowboy hats, Chinese children wear Red Army soldier caps to bring themselves closer to the adult world.

After we had left China, when Tiananmen Square blew up, however, I was not amazed.

Dong Kingman and Chin-San-Long had led me to expect brilliant art. I saw much excellent craftsmanship, all highly derivative of centuries past, but little personal approach to what we would call art. I saw no Chinese photography—none—although I made serious efforts to track it down. One museum was showing photography: it turned out to be Japanese Cibachromes. We did find one fascinating tile work in Xian, which we bought for our home, and it looks original—a scene of five cows in a circular composition. But perhaps there are a thousand such. I also found in the villages some delightful "peasant paintings," colorful primitives that projected an unmistakable sincerity. We admired rough stone sculptures in the Summer Palace—how very Chinese to have the patience to put a huge piece of limestone into a lake and wait twenty years for it to leach out into interesting shapes.

The hotel itself was immaculate, with excellent service, and we found (in contrast to dire warnings from friends) that the food was superb. My only discomfort was the condition of the few public toilets it was my misfortune to find it necessary to use. In the theatre, backstage, I once had the occasion to use the cast facilities, and to my amazement found them clean, orderly, and functioning. When I remarked to our No. 2 interpreter, lovely "Rainbow," that I was pleased with them, she giggled and admitted that they had been personally cleaned prior to our arrival by Bette Bao Lord, novelist wife of the American ambassador!

I was grateful that our hotel garden displayed several of those fascinating stone sculptures. At least Chuck had a few hours of quiet, sketching them in ink. The work at the theatre gripped him constantly with a determination to make the play work for a Chinese audience—would they really understand?

Opening night was a real moment of triumph for Chuck, for the actors, and for the author, Herman Wouk. When I saw the crowds surging into the theatre, I was astounded. I had been told that Chinese audiences were raucous, eating, drinking, and moving about during a performance, but during this one I listened mainly to their silence—to their rapt attention. They *did understand*.

I'm sure there is hope for that ancient and vivid country. I wish its people well.

CAINE/CHINA PROLOGUE
July 7, 1989

How did I end up in China, a few months before the bloody convulsion in Tiananmen Square, directing a Chinese cast in an American play, exploring the architecture of democracy? The classic answer serves: It seemed like a good idea at the time. Now it seems like an even better one.

At first, it was just on the list. In my line of work, you almost never know what you'll be doing four months down the line. There are several things you *might* do . . . if they get the right actress, if the script turns out, if it still seems like a good idea when you get to it. Actors are used to this . . . you take the best job that comes by.

I did a vastly expensive television series a few years ago, which the network suddenly canceled after two seasons. Much consternation in the press: "Why? What now? How do you feel, losing your job?" "Don't knock it," I said. "It's the longest job I've had since the 11th Air Force in World War II."

Nineteen eighty-seven and '88 were busy times: I spent six months on the London stage, playing Sir Thomas More in Robert Bolt's remarkable play, *A Man for All Seasons*. When we closed a record-breaking run in the spring, I seized the chance to make a film of it, directing most of the same cast, adding Vanessa Redgrave, John Gielgud, and Richard Johnson.

Directing and acting in a piece like *Man* is not "great fun," though journalists insist it must be. Samuel Johnson described it better when he said of a sentence of hanging, "It concentrates the mind wonderfully." (Mind you, Orson Welles said, "Directing a picture is the best set of electric trains any little boy ever had to play with.") That's true, too, and if you can't understand why, I can't explain it to you.

In the midst of all this, Jimmy Doolittle (a California producer who's done a lot, in fact) called me in London to ask if I'd be interested in directing a play in China.

"That'd be different," I said. "What play?"

"The Caine Mutiny Court-martial," Jimmy said. "In Chinese."

"Jimmy," I said, "you've got my attention. Why me, though? Why this play?"

"The Ministry of Culture knows your work," Jimmy said. "They know you've done *Caine Mutiny.* They want to give their theatre some experience in American realistic drama. This is the play they want to do, and they want you to direct it."

I thought about it overnight, then called him back. "You're one canny son of a bitch, pal," I said. "You knew damn well I couldn't let this go by. It's too tough and too interesting. I've got a film to do now, though. Will they wait?"

"They'll wait," he said. I turned back to *A Man for All Seasons.* Two weeks later, I came home to Los Angeles on some errand and seized the chance to lunch with Bette Bao Lord, a successful writer and the wife of Winston Lord, our ambassador to China. She's a very remarkable lady, positive and forceful. She's also a very striking woman, deeply informed, as a Chinese-American, on China and her people. She proved valuable beyond measure to *Caine*/China.

"The Chinese want this to happen," she said. "Particularly Ying Ruocheng. He's China's leading actor and the Vice Minister of Culture. He's behind us, all the way." Reassured, I disappeared into Tudor England and Sir Thomas More.

[Bette was dead right. Ying Ruocheng put the full weight of his personal authority and his creative capacity into our undertaking. Without him, *Caine* would never have sailed.]

We finished shooting *A Man for All Seasons* at the end of June and were ready to head home, waiting only for the Men's Final at Wimbledon, which I spent watching the rain from the Members' Enclosure, damply drinking white wine. It finally cleared enough for fifteen minutes of tennis in the dripping dusk. For the record, while I was flying home the next day, Edberg handily disposed of Becker.

God knows I was glad to *be* home. I make my living all over the world, sleeping in strange beds. One of the nice things about editing a film is that you can do it fifteen minutes from your own house. I've even done it *in* my own house. Well, in the screening room. I like that. By the end of the *Man* shoot, I needed it.

Editing is the most personal part of making a film, though it's hardly the lone artist working in ivory solitude. Film, unavoidably, is art by committee. (That's one of many reasons why it's so hard to make a good one.) When you're editing, though, the committee gets smaller: editor, producer, and director. On *Man,* there was Eric Boyd-Perkins, who's cut all the films I've directed and a couple I've acted in, and my son, Fraser, who's produced and written several of them. With Peter Snell, with whom I've also made several films, as executive producer, I felt in good hands. We're a seasoned, trusting team. You need that, crucially: to know that the other guy is not only talented and intelligent, but that he will tell you the truth.

Editing is also cheap time. When you're shooting, every day costs at least a hundred thousand dollars. If you stop during the working day to reexamine a choice you made on your own time at five o'clock that morning over coffee, your thinking costs several thousand dollars . . . if the sun clouds over while you're doing it, double that. But while you're editing, you're allowed to say, "Look, I'm not sure I *want* to go to the close-up as soon as he comes in the door. Let's put that aside for now and look at Reel 3."

This gave me time to think seriously about *The Caine Mutiny Court-martial*. I'd done Herman Wouk's play two years before, directing an American cast and acting the infamous Captain Queeg in my London stage debut. (A little long in the tooth for a debut.) It's a marvelous play; after closing a smashing West End season, we brought it home for runs in both Los Angeles and Washington, D.C.

Still, taking it to China was another thing. The play is set in World War II, defining the dimensions of democracy in terms of a military court-martial, focusing on the rights of the accused man. Communist governments view human rights very lightly. Could Chinese audiences understand, or care, what Wouk was talking about? Besides, I'm a known anti-Communist. Did they really want me to bring *Caine* to Beijing?

It seems they did. The Vice Minister of Culture, Ying Ruocheng, had endorsed the project, the play, and me as director. True, Communist governments won't *pay* you anything, but I'd sensed that from the beginning. I often work for nothing, though my Scottish ancestry and Depression upbringing draw the line at actually going in the hole on a project. Happily, the USIA (U.S. Information Agency) and some American companies agreed to cover our expenses.

Herman Wouk had enthusiastically granted the right for his play to be done in China. (I don't believe he was paid anything either.) In July, he drove up from Palm Springs with his wife, Sarah, to take part in a tumultuous press conference on the roof of my tennis pavilion, announcing our production of *The Caine Mutiny Court-martial*. The media, always capricious, decided we were hot. (I think it was a slow news week. Besides, it *was* kind of an unusual idea.) From that day forward, we were closely followed by the press. Not on the level of Elvis Presley sightings, of course, but we got our share of attention.

I'd hoped, before I took the final cut of *Man* to London for the scoring, dubbing, and final sound mix on the film, to take the long route by way of Beijing so I could cast *Caine* and discuss production . . . sets, lighting, and wardrobe. This just wasn't feasible. The cost of the trip, given the few days I'd have available in China, ruled it out. Instead, I sent fifteen pages of notes on the characters and sets. I got back very encouraging reports. The people on the other end knew what they were doing. It was clearly an offer I couldn't refuse. I turned the mix on *Man* over to Fraser and packed up for China.

CHINA JOURNAL, BOOK 1
9/14/88–9/18/88

SEPTEMBER 14th Wednesday L.A. to Beijing

Lydia and I landed in Beijing late Thursday, but only because we crossed the International Dateline sometime after midnight, still chasing the sun. I've never really understood how that works. Obviously the day has to start somewhere, but you feel no bump when you cross into tomorrow, westbound.

I was probably asleep anyway. We had a somewhat chaotic departure, our sixteen bags full of both needs and wants. (Clothes and peanut butter, rehearsal Reeboks and drawing pens . . . also the three-foot model of the *Caine* I'd had built for the production.) The limo was late, so I drove out in the pickup, bags bumbled in the back. We got to LAX in good time and were hand-carried from there, as I've come, irrationally, to count on.

My girl was in a lovely mood, though she woke me somewhere east of Tokyo in really rough air, hail rattling on the fuselage, needing to be held. When I did, she murmured Martha Gellhorn's line to Hemingway as he held her when they were being shelled in a Madrid hotel in the Spanish Civil War. "Being with you is like being in a blizzard . . . only the snow is warm." I was touched.

SEPTEMBER 15th Thursday Beijing

We landed late at night, met by Pat Corcoran, of the USIA at our embassy here, and Barbara Zigli, his number two. It's nice to see those red diplomatic passports at the plane door . . . friendly hands in the Communist wilderness at two in the morning. Driving in darkness to the hotel, we had only a glimpse of wide streets.

The Great Wall Hotel is an American Sheraton, putting us up on the cuff as a contribution to our cross-cultural venture. We had Chinese beer (Tsingtao, very good) in the hotel bar with the embassy people; my interpreter, Madame Xie; and Ren Ming, the assistant director from the People's Art Theatre who's prepared the cast for me. The conversation was not substantive, though Pat Corcoran had given me a concise and informed political overview as we drove in from the airport.

[In the light of the convulsions in China only months later, I wish I could say this included some speculation on the possible results of the major experiment the Chinese were undertaking in democracy and market economy. At the time, of course, they were moving far faster than the Soviets. In the event, too fast, perhaps, from their point of view. In any case, Pat did not explore this. Since he is one of the most informed sinologists I've ever met, he either didn't perceive the downside to what the West was cheering at the time, or he didn't feel it prudent to share his concerns with me.]

In the bar, we talked mostly about beer, exchanging our experience of it in different countries . . . in my case from

Argentina to Australia, Bangladesh to Norway, Scotland to South Africa. A clear consensus emerged: Perhaps alone among the works of man, almost all countries make a pretty good beer. No, not paintings or poems; the good stuff there is harder to find. But with the exception of the French, who don't really care about beer and probably feel they could do it if they wanted to, and the Soviets, who have too many other things on their minds, everybody makes good beer. That world issue settled, we checked into a room already inundated with our luggage, and fell into bed and the sleep of the just and jet-lagged.

SEPTEMBER 16th Friday People's Art Theatre Rehearsal Day #1

I woke early (I always do, however many time zones I've jumped—it's either all these years of 5:00 AM calls on film locations, or just my dour Scot's rectitude) and looked out every window, hoping to see . . . the Great Wall itself? At least the Forbidden City? No, only a vast expanse of buildings, stretching into the morning distance. There were classic hutongs, lined with tile-roofed huts in walled compounds, many Western-style buildings, and a surprising number of high rises punctuating the skyline.

I went down on the grounds and wandered a bit. Tennis courts (I hope I have time) and an extraordinary garden with examples of all the things you expect to see in China, including a model section of the Great Wall. If your trip doesn't leave time to go to all these places, you can photograph reasonable facsimiles thereof right outside the hotel.

Then, before going to the theatre, I had a quick coffee with Winston Lord, our ambassador here, and his wife, Bette, whom I'd already met with in L.A. Both were most warm and forthcoming, though he obviously has a larger agenda than our little undertaking, of which she, I think, is the prime architect. She's also a successful writer of formidable creative and cultural credentials, flawlessly expert in both English and Mandarin. In addition, she's a volcano of energy. I do believe I'll need all the help she can give me.

Taking a deep breath, I eased into rehearsals an hour later at the People's Art Theatre, a large, somewhat dusty complex built in 1955, with a theatre a lot like the Ahmanson in L.A., including the formidable apron and orchestra pit separating the audience from the stage. (Someone said, "Standing on the Ahmanson's forestage is like acting Shakespeare on the cliffs of Dover . . . only the audience is in France!"

God knows I've had ample experience with *that* problem; I've acted in the Ahmanson in more plays than anyone else. East is East and West is West, but we can both design flawed theatres, apparently.

My introduction to the theatre and the company I'll be working with for the next month or so was eased by the formidable presence of Ying Ruocheng, one of China's most distinguished actors. (Film-goers remember his chilling performance as the inquisitor in *The Last Emperor*.) During the Cultural Revolution of the '60s, he was rendered a "nonperson," to use a Soviet phrase.

Solzhenitsyn describes in *The Gulag Archipelago* the range of indignities, humiliations, abominations, and murders visited on Russians labeled as nonpersons. I have no idea, nor did Ying Ruocheng ever mention, what his punishment was. Many, many thousands of Chinese were simply exiled for years of work, tending pigs or making bricks (without straw, no doubt). Many, many thousands more died. He survived. Toughness counts, I would think.

Now, his reputation restored, Ying Ruocheng is Vice Minister of Culture. Approval of our project in general, deciding which American play to do and the invitation to me to direct it was crucially his. For good measure, Ruocheng personally translated the play into Mandarin. Bespectacled and burly, he also presided genially over the read-through of the play I assembled this morning.

It was considerably more than that, in fact. In a large, high-ceilinged rehearsal room only fifty yards down the hall from the stage itself, they've set up a very creditable rehearsal set, with doors and stairs and furniture . . . much more complete than IATSE (our stagehands' union in the U.S.) would ever let us rehearse in back home.

They showed me a run-through of the play as they've prepared it so far. Unbelievably, almost all the actors know almost all their lines. Even the blocking's been sketched in . . . an absolute first in my experience as a director (or as an actor, for that matter). **["Blocking" means deciding where the actors stand on the stage, and when and how they get there. Why they call this "blocking," I have no idea. Shakespeare probably coined it when he was directing the first Hamlet. "No, you whoreson blockhead! Over THERE!"]**

Meeting the actors was an interesting experience. I've never before come to the first day of rehearsal not knowing one member of the cast. We stood on tiptoe staring at each other over the language barrier, smiling anxiously. I doubt they'd ever heard my name. ("Who's this big round-eye? Why is he directing us?") I know they've heard of *Ben-Hur* and *The Ten Commandments,* but no foreign film made since 1949 has ever been shown commercially in China. With the help of the invaluable Mme. Xie, I hope I made them understand something of the excitement and challenge I feel at trying to make this play work here, with them.

The casting, based on my character notes and the photographs and résumés they sent me while I was in England, seems right. The actors are clearly disciplined, motivated, and very well trained. To say more than that, I need to know them better than I do, but I was enormously encouraged by what I saw. A couple of them are a bit young for their roles, a couple a bit old, but you always get that disparity with a repertory company. This one is supposed to be the best in China. I can believe it. Ren Ming, my tall, lean assistant, has done a superb job with the actors. While they have no experience of Western acting, they know the traditional Chinese style is somewhat more formal. They understand we're going to explore a looser approach, and they all have concepts of their roles clear enough to begin work.

We didn't do that today, of course. The actors seemed keen to start, but it doesn't hurt to let that edge build a little. I let them go home and turned to the technicians (often a thorny bunch, anywhere in the world). These seemed OK,

Cong Lin (left) as Keith, the young lieutenant whose testimony against Captain Queeg is discredited by prosecutor Challee (Wu Guiling), listens uneasily as Chuck's direction is translated into Mandarin by Mme. Xie, the company interpreter. Her lightning facility in the two languages was a tremendous advantage to the entire production, and Chuck's confidence in the project took wings on the first day.

though the lighting man had many anxieties, particularly about his equipment. "Some of it is forty years old!"

"My equipment's a hell of a lot older than that," I said. "We'll manage." They are, understandably, very sensitive to their lack of modern technology. As someone (Shaw?) said, "All you really need for theatre is two planks and a passion." (That can be hard to come by, too.)

Never mind. They all seem determined to serve the play as well as they can, which is what I have in mind.

SEPTEMBER 17th Saturday Rehearsal Day #2

We began this morning by reworking the blocking my assistant, Ren Ming, has provided. He's affably intense, taller than most Chinese, and skinnier than most men. What he's done so far with the cast and the play is good. Just to be able to begin work on a scene and have the actors moving and speaking more or less appropriately gives you a lot of foundation to build on.

The main problem for me, as I knew from the start, is language. I have two interpreters, one a pretty young woman with a dazzling smile who does messages and phone calls . . . a bilingual gofer, I suppose. Her name is very difficult to pronounce, so we settled on an English approximation that seemed to amuse her: Miss Rainbow. Then there's Mme. Xie (no, that's *not* so hard to pronounce: you just start to say "X" and switch to "Zhee"), an extraordinary lady with wise eyes and lightning facility in switching from English to Mandarin and back. Her composure suggests how she endured what she went through in the Cultural Revolution (along with millions of her countrymen, of course). Since then, most of her work has been translating American plays. I was awed by her facility at a press conference at the hotel this morning before rehearsal, watching her flick back and forth from Mandarin to French and English. She's a remarkable lady. I could hardly have a better tongue to reach my actors.

As Arthur Miller told me **[the first American to direct a play in China; he was most gracious in describing his experience at length to me over the phone, which I fleshed out later with his excellent book]**, when he was doing *Death of a Salesman* here, he found that you really don't have trou-

Keeping the members of the court alive and involved was one of the major difficulties (see the alert characters on the right!).

ble keeping track of where the actors are in a scene. If you're an actor, you damn sure don't. To me, the sequence of the lines, who's speaking, the way he sounds—even in Chinese —makes it perfectly clear where we are and what I want to do about it.

But I can't take notes and wait till the scene's over. Most of the time, directing, there are bits you're more or less happy with from the start . . . you can turn your mind to other things while they're going on. (I have *got* to talk to Maryk about his hair . . . do I really have to pee now? Naah, wait till lunch.) Here, I have to watch the actors and the English text in front of me every second, to be sure I know what I'm looking at. It's a formidable exercise in concentration.

It also means I have to stop and comment every time I

Li Guangfu as Signalman Urban. After an initial attempt to play the terrified young sailor as a country bumpkin, Li found his character by playing seriously, and therefore in a vastly more human and touchingly funny way.

see something questionable, or want to change something. I don't dare wait till the end of the scene. The actors are marvelously patient with this, and surprisingly directable. In twenty minutes work, I was able to make the rest of the company—who can serve as a surrogate audience in rehearsal—laugh at Urban. **[Urban is a twenty-year-old signalman . . . a country boy who's called to testify as to what** happened on the bridge of the *Caine* during the typhoon when Lieutenant Maryk relieved Queeg of command. The last thing in the world he wants to do is get anyone in trouble . . . especially himself. It's an hilarious scene. In the London production, I'd cast a very good young English actor as Urban, dyed his blond hair red and taught him an accurate Georgia accent. (In World War II, there were a lot of Southerners in the Navy.) For the American production, I found a Southern actor who was actually redheaded. In China, of course, neither redheaded nor Georgian was a possible option. Urban was played by Li Guangfu, a fresh-faced youngster who was very good, once he understood the part.] Today, he was trying to be funny in the scene, which is not the way to do it. Urban is a farm boy out of his depth and scared; his aim in the scene is to stay out of trouble . . . *thus* he is funny. Noel Coward, who sure Lord knew, said it: All comic scenes must be played very seriously.

We did well, working about halfway through the first act (by far the longer of the two) by the end of the day. **[Some directors like to begin by having the actors sit around a table, reading the play. While this is a reasonable tradition, I've never found it terribly useful. It certainly won't help me to hear the text read in Chinese at this point. I need to keep the actors on their feet, moving through the scenes. That's when I can find out about them and the men they play. That's what we began today.]**

I was tired when I got back to the hotel, but since I sleep on planes (my innate purity of heart) I wasn't really jet-lagged, even with the fifteen-hour time change. Lydia brought Maggie Field (a loved and longtime friend, visiting us from Paris) in from the airport, and we went off to dinner at the U.S. Embassy Residence. Of course, the taxi took us first to the North Vietnamese Embassy, which I somehow recognized instantly, from the guards at the gate, though I haven't been in Vietnam since when . . . '71? If I'd gotten out of the taxi, I might still be inside, which would be very annoying for Lydia, not to mention the People's Art Theatre.

Of course, it hasn't been that long since George Bush took over the old Pakistani Embassy as our first envoy here since 1949. The taxi driver finally found it, and the Lords gave us a fine evening. They strike me as very well equipped to represent us here.

SEPTEMBER 18th Sunday Day Off

We had an easy day, which I needed. After lying around the suite all morning (not quite as relaxing as lying around the ridge back home), Pat Corcoran, who has the USIA film program I'm doing here on his plate, drove us out to the Forbidden City, which I remember well from when we captured it in *55 Days in Peking*. Colesanti and Moore did a lovely job designing that set . . . the real one looks exactly like it. There is vastly more of it here, of course, with the patina of centuries and the smell of history ingrained in those curved tile roofs. It was odd to find it so familiar.

What I find in the real Forbidden City, which even Sam Bronston's unstinting profligacy in *55 Days* couldn't provide, is a relentlessly *increasing* grandeur as you progress through vast courtyards, each bigger than the one before; the steps to the building at the far end longer, higher; each building a larger temple to the unspeakable glory of the Emperor, still unseen, unknowable, beyond still larger courtyards, higher steps, grander temples, stretching immeasurably beyond belief. What did it seem like to Marco Polo at the end of a year of struggling across Asia, or the first British envoy two centuries later, to walk alone through the beating drums for almost a mile of this? It's no wonder the Empire lasted so many thousand years . . . or that the reaction against it was so bloody.

I like the Corcorans; both Pat and his wife, Renata, are deeply intelligent, committed people. They care about what they're doing. It's very reassuring to know there are people of that quality serving us around the world. When not actually making a living, I've spent a little part of my life charging around for the Foreign Service on one errand or another.

Pat Corcoran, First Secretary of the American Embassy, and his wife, Renata, provided many an amusing interlude in their apartment in the foreign quarter of Beijing. Pat's ability to maneuver easily in Mandarin and his consistent good humor about our whole mad undertaking reinforced us both. Pat and Renata (now stationed in Italy) filled their home with superb Chinese antiques and "peasant" paintings. Our admiration for them is boundless.

(Thirty-odd countries, Lydia says. I think less.) Every damn time you step off a plane, or a boat, or a jeep in the ass-end of nowhere, there's someone like Pat Corcoran standing there to make sure you don't make a jerk of yourself (or get shot, which comes to the same thing). I don't buy the Graham Greene burnt-out-case scenario. There are good men and women like the Corcorans all over the world, trying to make the whole bloody thing work. God bless them and all they love.

When we got back to the hotel, their in-house computer guru (an affable New Zealander named Kevin King) had been working for an hour to get Igor (my portable computer, a cranky brute) working on local power. Igor was sullenly silent, but Kevin remained undaunted. "Never mind . . . get it tomorrow." It occurs to me that Aussies and Kiwis are probably constitutionally required to be undaunted. Not a bad idea. We used to be that way, too.

CHINA JOURNAL, BOOK 2
9/19/88–9/25/88

SEPTEMBER 19th Monday Rehearsal Day #3

We're beginning to settle into the routine of rehearsals now, immensely aided by the full rehearsal set, with furniture and practical doors we'd never be allowed at home. They've also found me a huge upholstered chair with dragons on the arms, in which I'll be spending most of the next few weeks, watching *Caine Mutiny* come alive. It vastly enhances the image of the director as God. I need all of that I can get.

Mme. Xie sits at my left, with a narrow table in front of us, holding her Mandarin text and my prompt script from the London production. She runs a pencil point down the English text as it plays in Mandarin, so I can check what line's being spoken, if I lose track of it, watching the actors.

I can't join in the usual easy banter that marks the time before every rehearsal, all over the world, all the way back to Richard Burbage kidding Shakespeare. ("Will, do you really want me to do that stupid 'To be, or not to be' crap? You can do better than that, forsooth.") Here in Beijing, I don't know what they're *saying!* I can't ask Mme. Xie to translate the actors' prerehearsal morning jokes, for God's sake.

This language barrier mandates a somewhat more formal actor/director relationship than I'm used to. The actors seem comfortable with it, and I see no other way. I make sure I'm the first in the rehearsal room, of course, and sit reading my *International Herald Tribune* till it's time to begin. (It's a curiously naive paper, politically, but I've read it working in six continents for forty years, grateful for good wire service coverage, football scores, and *Peanuts.*)

There's the tea, too . . . far more important to the Chinese than the *Tribune,* I expect. On my right is a round, low table (also with dragons, but smaller ones) for my mug, handsomely painted porcelain. When I come in the morning, the cup's waiting, a quarter full of dry tea leaves. Someone instantly fills it with very hot water and keeps it so all day. I never see anyone adding either water or fresh leaves, but the tea's always strong, black, and *there*. I don't even *like* tea, particularly, but this does the job.

[I didn't notice till some days later that, while all the actors had personal tea mugs, most of them were Nescafé jars insulated with personalized string wrapping. These guys are actors in the most distinguished company in China and they're bicycling to work and drinking tea out of instant coffee jars. Socialism at work.]

We did well today, getting through Act I. It means we've blocked over half the play in two working days. Of course, I remind myself that Ren Ming gave me the play rough-blocked, with the cast having learned most of their parts. Good for them, by God.

We do have a problem. On Friday, the play ran some forty minutes longer than it ever did in the English or American productions I directed. Two hours and fifty-some minutes is too long for this play **[or just about anything this side of *Lear*]**. There's also this: The buses in Beijing stop running at ten. The audience will walk out on our last scene if the curtain's not down well ahead of that. Believe me, this fact has caught my attention. The play will stand cuts. Any play will. I've cut Shakespeare and O'Neill every time I've done them . . . and Wouk, for that matter, when I first did this play in London. We took out a bit under two minutes then, with Herman's approval. I think it helped us. It'll be harder to get more than that out here without losing something valuable. Let's try.

[As I review these pages from my Beijing journal, I've just

Cong Lin is beginning to understand a little English as Chuck demonstrates what he wants in Cong's performance. Mme. Xie, always intent and alert, strains to connect actor and director. Her command of English was quite impressive; in fact, her only question on English usage was, "What is the difference between piss *and* pee?" *Chuck had to think that one over.*

come back from nine solid hours in a cutting room on the fourth work-through, reel by reel, shot by shot, of my current film. (No, *A Man for All Seasons* was last year. This is *Treasure Island,* and my son's directing, not I. Otherwise, the team's the same, including a lot of the actors.) Editing a film, or cutting a play, consists of taking out the not-so-good bits so the good bits come closer together. A thousand points of light, if you like, though, this side of Shakespeare, that's very hard to come by. You're always faced with hard choices, like the Beijing buses. That's what we were dealing with.]

SEPTEMBER 20th Tuesday Rehearsal Day #4

We moved ahead easily today, finishing the last half of Act I by lunch and taking Act II through the Queeg breakdown. I'm amazed at how easy it is . . . and how useful . . . just to step into a scene and play it in English, while the other actors play in Mandarin. "Please watch," I say. "Let me be you." (I've learned how to say this in Mandarin.)

I know the script almost verbatim, of course, and the scenes are there. It's hard to explain; I'd never have guessed it, but it works . . . wonderfully. It also lets me leap over the language barrier and reach the actors directly, *doing* for them what I mean, rather than have the estimable Mme. Xie tell them what I mean.

True, I have to do this by acting it with them, unavoidably *giving them readings*. When I was studying at Northwestern (God, we were all so *sure,* then. We were seventeen and we *knew!*), they sent you to directing jail for giving an actor a reading. In fact, since I'm acting the scene in a different language, what I give them is not a "reading," but the body temperature of the line, the chemistry of the character . . . which is exactly what I want to give them. I look into the other actor's eyes and we're communicating, man to

Chuck found that he could play a scene in English with the other actors performing in Mandarin, and communicate the basic sense of the characters' objectives. Soon he discovered that he could understand the lines in Chinese. This was a tremendous help to everyone.

man. The language disappears. This is working. It makes me very happy.

I remember working for Willy Wyler on *The Big Country*, in a scene with Carroll Baker, fresh from Lee Strasberg and The Actors Studio. Willy was the best director of performance I ever saw, but he was a little skeptical about the whole idea of acting as an art form. He dealt with it sort of pragmatically, like fixing a watch. He himself couldn't act at all, of course, but he told Carroll what he wanted her to emphasize in a speech. She recoiled, amazed. "Willy, . . ." she said. "Are you giving me a reading? You want me to *play* it that way?"

"That's right," he said. "I'm the director. That's what they pay me for . . . to get you to do it the way I want it." Yes, I know, that sounds a little harsh. Most of us come at it a little differently now. Willy was right, though. In the end, Carroll was absolutely superb in the scene.

[Some years later, when the American Film Institute gave Willy the Life Achievement Award, we found that actors working under his direction had earned some forty Academy nominations and more than a dozen awards, far more than any other director. So much for the dangers of giving actors readings.]

SEPTEMBER 21st Wednesday Rehearsal Day #5

By lunchtime today, I finished blocking the play. That's the whole piece, in three-and-a-half days. I'm pleased, not least because it gives me a chance to address the time cuts we need *now*, when we need to make them.

I spent most of the morning on the end . . . the party scene. It's a problem, the only part of the play that dates a little; yet, in Greenwald's closing speech, it makes Wouk's central point: In the crucial crisis in the history of the 20th century, ". . . when Earth's foundations trembled . . . ," who stood in the breach? The slim cadre of trained professionals that formed the core of our tiny peacetime armed forces. These were the men who commanded the regiments, led the squadrons, captained the ships, and fought a holding action while they turned a mass of drafted civilians into the fighting force that won the war. These were Wouk's "poor old regulars," including quirky misfits like Queeg.

This is the point Robert Altman studiously avoided making in his curious version of the play for TV last year, but it's Wouk's point. I'm determined to make it here, even for Chinese audiences that may be uncertain what he means about "keeping my old Jewish mama from being melted down to a bar of soap."

Nevertheless, in Chinese, we still need cutting. I can barely order breakfast in Mandarin, but I begin to sense its formal intricacies. Mme. Xie, Bette Lord, and I spent the afternoon at the U.S. Residency, working through the second act. The cast is far ahead of where they need to be now. We can spare the time. We need to do it. Carefully.

Lydia and Maggie joined me at the Residency for lunch, then they went to tour the Summer Palace (where the Dow-

Our lovely friend Maggie, who came out from Paris, found the Corcorans' home full of joie de vivre. Chuck, although he devoured Chinese food with gusto (with the possible exception of sea slugs), is here demonstrating his pleasure at a real American meal.

ager Empress of China fled after I chased her out of Peking in *55 Days*). Meantime, I sat down with Bette Lord and Mme. Xie to whittle away at the Chinese complexities that have somehow crept into the translation. **[Sandpapering is more like it, stroke by stroke.]** It may be that Vice Minister Ruocheng's translation uses a more formal literary style. I can't tell. There're traces of that in Wouk's play, for that matter. We just have to be sure it doesn't compound in our Chinese text. It's an interesting problem.

SEPTEMBER 22nd Thursday Day Off

With a film, if things go well and you gain time on the schedule, that gain's clear and risk-free . . . you put it in the bank against a rainy day, a recalcitrant actress, or a scene gone wrong. The scene you got ahead on waits patiently in those little rolls of film on the cutting room shelves, till you finish the shooting and put it all together.

A play doesn't work that way. The performances are not sitting on a shelf, waiting to be edited; they're churning around inside the actors, straining for shape and coherence, thrusting toward that last orgasmic surge of certainty. It can be like that, believe me. Acting can be better than sex.

Ideally, this comes just before the opening, after a flawed final dress rehearsal, when you can't wait for opening night because you *know* you've got it at last. The director has to help this happen. He also has to make sure it doesn't come too soon.

It's like a coach training a runner up to his peak condition for the day of the race . . . or a quarterback, or a boxer. I know, acting's not a competition, but in a sense it *is*. The actor competes with himself . . . with what is in him and in the part. If he finds that too soon, he can go slack. That's why you should never go to a play the second night of its run. You'll very often get a loose performance, far below the opening night level.

That's why I gave the company the day off. They're well along toward getting technical control of their parts. I want to be sure they don't peak too soon. The script needs more work . . . the *Chinese* script. It still plays too long, especially in the longer speeches.

Lovely "Rainbow," the assistant interpreter-guide, who made Maggie's and my days in Beijing much more exciting than they might have been had we moseyed around on our own.

I took advantage of my day off (after working on the script in the morning) to join Lydia and Maggie in a trip to the Great Wall. I suppose this is the one absolutely obligatory sight in all China, as it must've been for the thousands of years it's stretched for hundreds of miles across this huge land, keeping out the savages. Hadrian's Wall pales beneath it. You stand on the twisting line of ramparts, looking north, and think yourself behind the eyes of a soldier standing through the snow in winter and the rain in summer centuries ago, waiting for the surge of screaming men to scramble up the slope with swords against him. In the end, the Mongols got over and ruled China for two centuries. What did old G. Washington say? "Eternal vigilance is the price of liberty." Hard to do. Hard to do.

SEPTEMBER 23rd Friday Rehearsal Day #6

Starting again from the top, I thought we'd move much faster today. We didn't. Between clarifying the text and working on performances, by the end of the day we got only a little further than we did the first day of rehearsal . . . the Keith scene.

The Chinese text is still a problem. We have more than enough time to work on performances, and I've also arm-wrestled the sets and wardrobe people, as well as lights and sound and props to about where they should be. Now it's time to make further cuts in the thickets of Mandarin blooming in every scene.

The actors are making a heroic effort as it is. Four or five of the principals are performing at night in another play. To rehearse one play by day and play another at night? I haven't done that since summer stock in Pennsylvania in '47! I told them to go home a little early and asked the actors playing the heaviest roles—the judge, the prosecutor, the defendant and his attorney, and Queeg—to come back in the morning ready to work through Act I around a table, finding ways to straight-line the Chinese text. I can only do this with their help. Lacking the language, all I have is my ear, telling me when a line plays long, or wrong.

On the way back to the hotel, I watched the Beijing traffic. It's a problem, but very different from New York's or London's. For one thing, it's mostly bicycles. Swarms, shoals, migrations of bicycles. There are streets with separate bicycle lanes; most of the Beijing streets are very wide. One of the major avenues occupies the ground where the city wall once stood, torn down shortly after the triumph of the '49 revolution. I'm told they wish they hadn't done that

Dear Mr. Li! Our driver was always calm and confident, something of an achievement in the wild streets of bicycle land. He told us how he had been arbitrarily assigned to driving—no career choice is available to most Chinese—but he was happy in his little Shanghai, with no complaints. I was particularly impressed with his skill at night, when wraithlike bicycles would suddenly dash into the very dark streets from right or left through the Beijing fog, slipping past our fenders like two-wheeled ghosts.

now. It's considerably wider than Park Avenue, but still the cyclists challenge the cars constantly (mostly trucks and vans, really . . . there are almost no private cars in Beijing; now *there's* an idea for New York . . . no private cars!!). The cyclists are as bold as bandits, pedaling firmly on a converging course, carefully avoiding eye contact. This means that the motor traffic moves at a very moderate pace, ready to brake if a bicycle fails to give ground in the end. This isn't a terrible idea, I suppose, but I'm used to being on the other end of the competition, matching wits with an eighteen

Bicycles and buildings—construction was under way everywhere. Wondering why there were so many apparently empty apartment buildings when the city was bursting with new edifices, we asked Mme. Xie to explain. She laughed and told us, "Those are apartments reserved by older people so that eventually their grandchildren will have a place to live. Now they will stay empty for some years."

We did not see the interior of a single Chinese dwelling place, a fact we can't explain. Perhaps they felt their quarters were too modest to show to foreigners, or perhaps they cling to the final shred of privacy available to them. Perhaps.

wheeler on the Hollywood Freeway at sixty miles an hour, not worrying about a kid on a bike doing ten.

I'm glad I have a good driver . . . Mr. Li. (Mme. Xie tells me that the Chinese almost never use their first names . . . a custom I'm comfortable with.) He drives a car made in China in 1982, one of the few passenger models produced here. It's called the Shanghai. (Funny, General Motors never did put out a car called the Detroit.) It's a pale ice blue and looks a lot like a '59 Oldsmobile. There are no seat belts. I sit in the front seat, Mme. Xie and any other passengers in the back, because I have more leg room (though not enough . . . it can be tough to be tall). Mr. Li spent several years shoveling pig shit during the Cultural Revolution. I can't imagine what he could have done to arouse the ire of the Red Guard (though I gather that was not difficult). He's a cheerful man, apparently unmarked by his experience. I expect he remembers it, though.

SEPTEMBER 24th Saturday Rehearsal Day #7

Editing

Once more from the top, line by line, reading the play. I *hate* read-throughs . . . I never do them, but it's the only way to deal with this problem. Our Chinese text still explores points Wouk's already made *clear*. We have to get them out. We can do it.

When I got back to the hotel, there was a letter from Mike Dormer of Thames TV, announcing his boss had finally opted out of the TV project. **[I'd been approached by a British company about doing a documentary on our China production. They were very enthusiastic about the idea, but in the end, it fell through. Happens all the time. In film, there are always three or four reasons not to do a project, and seldom more than one to do it. Saying "no" is always safer . . . and cheaper.]** I wasn't surprised, really, nor terribly disappointed. In this trade, you learn to deal with rejection, God knows. Besides, when I get home, I can devote what energy I have in this area toward a small book on the *Caine* in China. **[And here I am, some months later, doing the book.]** Meantime, I have to get the bloody boat in the water.

SEPTEMBER 25th Sunday Day Off

We're still digging at the Mandarin text . . . tough, finicky work. The English text will bear some cutting, too . . . not scenes, or speeches . . . just the leanest way to say it. I believe this helps the play, in either language. Oddly, I think some of the cuts we're making here to accommodate the intricacies of Mandarin could've intensified the way the play worked in London, or Washington. Herman Wouk might not agree with me . . . but then again, he might. He's an extraordinary man.

Anyway, none of this happened today. It's my day off! I didn't open the script. (I thought about it.) I played my first tennis in two weeks, with a boundlessly energetic and amiable Burmese pro named Arthur, then I went with Lydia and Maggie to see the Lamasery Temple.

The history of all this is complicated and marvelously Chinese. In essence, it's a former palace which turned out to be the birthplace of a future (18th century) emperor, whereupon it was abandoned as a palace and became the center of the Lamaist faith. This is all very important politically to the People's Republic, so the temple is meticulously maintained. On a smaller scale than the Forbidden City, but somehow more accessible. (Also a shorter tour and closer to the center of Beijing.) I was glad to have time to make a few sketches, even happier to be back at the hotel early, so we could relax a bit and dawdle over deciding where we'd eat.

[There were several very good restaurants, all in Western hotels. Unlike other Communist countries, the Chinese take food very seriously. I don't mean feeding their people (none of them does that very well), but how it actually

tastes. The Chinese manage that superbly. In our hotel alone, there were two Chinese restaurants (Szechuan and Cantonese), a French restaurant, and an American restaurant, which during October converted to German cuisine to celebrate Oktoberfest. Another hotel had a very fine Italian restaurant we sometimes went to.

Still, we never ate anywhere but in an American hotel, the U.S. Embassy Residence, or the Corcorans' apartment. During rehearsals, I lunched alone in my dressing room at the theatre. True, both my interpreters and I needed a daily break from high-jumping back and forth over the language barrier. It's also true that foreigners are almost never invited to private homes in France, for instance, but I've since come to realize there were other pressures at work in China.

We'd thought it would be interesting to have a meal at an ordinary local Beijing restaurant. This idea was not greeted enthusiastically. Yes, it was certainly possible, I was told: The selected restaurant would simply clear the Chinese customers from a room and serve us there. This seemed like a lousy idea to me, so we abandoned it. I now think, though, that the conflicts that reached flash point a few months later in Tiananmen Square had already been perceived.

The Chinese, remember, were running a very advanced civilization when the rest of us were painting ourselves blue and building Stonehenge. When Rome fell, they were already entrepreneurs . . . they were delighted to meet Marco Polo. But market economy is a grass that'll flourish anywhere; poor Papa Marx has tried to chop it out through the whole of the 20th century. Democracy, on the other hand, is a fragile Western flower . . . easily crushed by tyrants. The Chinese were capitalists before they were Communists. From the perspective of some months later, I have no doubt the government in Beijing was thinking hard about all this before we got there.]

CHINA JOURNAL, BOOK 3
9/26/88–10/18/88

Zhu Xu (the maddening and pitiful Captain Queeg) checks out a confusing line with Mme. Xie while Chuck, mightily pleased at last to find himself on the real set, looks on.

SEPTEMBER 26th Monday Rehearsal Day #8

Cutting Text

We didn't rehearse today. I sat with the principal actors, Ren Ming, and Mmes. Xie and Lord, still cutting Chinese text. The problem's not just getting the audience on the last buses . . . but the sound of a speech in my ear. I know what it says in English and how it serves the scene. If it takes too long in Mandarin, it won't work. I *know* this in my bones.

When a speech runs long as the actor speaks, I look for dispensable phrases, adjectives, adverbs (articles are gone anyway; Mandarin's very short on articles). The Chinese are good at finding useful Mandarin slang. No surprise. Actors know how to do this.

Still, it was a long day. I have to keep one eye on the English text and one ear alert to the sound in Chinese. (For one thing, my eyes get tired.) Cutting text is not my favorite part of play-making. For dinner tonight, I had what turned out to be sea slugs. I wasn't too crazy about them either.

SEPTEMBER 27th Tuesday Rehearsal Day #9

Work Through Act I

We finally got back to actually staging the play! Working through Act I, I was glad to see that several of the actors seem quite happy to be called by the names of their characters. (Many Chinese names are hard to pronounce; you must also remember that only the last names are used . . . like the Brits, come to think of it: "Look here, Masterson.") Lundeen, Bird, and Southard, then, are very close to what I want with their parts. (I must be careful not to let them get too close, too soon.)

Some of the others have a little further to go. There's a different sense of tempo, I'm told, in the Chinese theatre. While PAT (the People's Art Theatre, who invited me here) has a stronger tradition of realism than the other theatres in China, there's still a certain tendency simply to demonstrate the appropriate emotion, underlined a little. I want something different here, and I think they do, too. Ren Baoxian, who's playing Greenwald (the defense attorney created by Henry Fonda and the protagonist of the play), understands this very well. He's a very good actor, maybe the best I have. He's not as tall as Hank and of course lacks his quintessential American quality. (What other actors *did* have that . . . Gary Cooper . . . Jimmy Stewart?) But Baoxian projects the wry, gritty decency you need in Greenwald. He'll be very good. I'd bet the farm on it.

He's moving very surely to where I want him to be in a couple of weeks. Wu Guiling, the actor playing the prosecuting attorney, Lieutenant Commander Challee, is doing less well. He's having trouble with his lines and remember-

Wu Guiling, Chuck, Ren Baoxian, and Mme. Xie change a bit of blocking to clarify the action.

ing his moves. I'm told this is the largest part he's played so far; he may be a little daunted by the prospect. He shouldn't be, of course. For any actor, the first good part you get should be raw meat tossed to a tiger. Never mind . . . we'll bring him to it.

[The People's Art Theatre was determined to explore Western traditions of realism in performance; that's why I was asked to come and do this play. The actors responded marvelously, but, within a few months, this creative freedom ground to a bloody halt under the tanks in Tiananmen Square. Many things were lost there; I suppose one company of actors working in a different way was the least important. Still, I'm sorry it's gone. I guess it'll be a long time before a Chinese company acts again "in the Western manner."]

On the way home, I stopped in at an exhibit of modern Chinese sculpture. It was essentially a photo op for the sculptor, which was fine with me. The capitalist road comes to China; I'm all for it. I liked his work . . . deriving, he said, from primitive Chinese cultures seven thousand years old. Now that's an *old* civilization. In that context, Lexington and Concord happened the day before yesterday . . . though never doubt how they defined us. [Perhaps the Chinese carry the fierce imperatives of that ancient culture, still drifting in the blood, looming in the distant, dusty shadows behind them, to show, sharp-toothed, last June.]
I got back to the hotel to find that my girl had succumbed to some intestinal bug. I showed the flag alone at a reception at the hotel, then on to dinner at the Pakistani Embassy. I was glad to get a knowledgeable briefing on the Afghan situation, including an assessment of the assassination of President Zia. Indian or KGB? Probably the Soviets, said the ambassador. Yeah . . . probably.

Ren Baoxian (playing the Henry Fonda role of attorney Greenwald) registers the three-way translation—director-to-interpreter-to-actor. Baoxian played Greenwald with superb timing and intensity. He surprised us on the night before first dress rehearsal, when we saw a delightful, ironic play about Chinese life, Baoxian showing us a light touch we hadn't expected. The performers of the People's Art Theatre (with a lifetime of training and, I'm afraid, minimal remuneration) are bringing a fresh breath of naturalism to the Chinese scene.

SEPTEMBER 28th Wednesday Rehearsal Day #10

We couldn't rehearse this morning because of a morning performance of the company's current play. I'd never heard of such a thing. Run-throughs, yes, or previews, but performances? It turns out that in China, factories or commercial companies often buy out a whole performance of a play and give their workers tickets for a morning performance on a working day. They thus get a morning off work and the show as well. (I wonder how many give away the tickets and just stay home for the morning with their feet up? Never mind, it's still a good idea. On the other hand, the actors have to work early. As John F. Kennedy pointed out, who said life was fair?)

I took advantage of the easy day (we didn't work in the afternoon either, so the actors who were in the morning performance could rest) to get through a chunk of paperwork and a good sweaty hit on the hotel courts with a fine young American player, who probably doesn't realize that he shares the name (if not quite the game) of a Top Ten American just after World War II: Dick Savitt. This Savitt's posted here for the *L.A. Times* and not only speaks but writes Chinese. All this and a neat topspin backhand.

We had only a two-and-a-half-hour session tonight, but I worked the actors halfway through Act II pretty effectively. Xiao Peng, who plays Maryk, understands now that his testimony here consists essentially of telling his stories about Queeg's disordered behavior: the coffee silex, the cowardice at Kwajalein, the stolen strawberries, the typhoon. Greenwald has him tell the court about these incidents because, though Maryk's not an articulate man, he was shaken by them and speaks with undeniable honesty. Each story is really a little two-minute play by itself. Actors . . . *all* actors, from time to time . . . tend to find a color, a point of view, for a character and simply play that in every scene. You have to find out what the scene's about first, then deal with that.

Contrary to the beliefs of the activist playwrights, real people seldom change their basic convictions . . . who they *are*. In the best play I know in the last quarter century, Robert Bolt's *A Man for All Seasons,* nobody alters an iota . . . not More, not the king, certainly not the common man. Only Rich changes, in every scene, as he declines into betrayal and perjury. That's the point of his character, really . . . that he has none. In *Caine,* as in any good play, the task is to define the character, then respond to the thrust of the different pressures the play puts on him. But the characters *remain the same.*

In the real world, for example, though I, along with several million other Americans, abandoned my early support and passionate belief in F.D.R. and Adlai Stevenson and Jack Kennedy, it was not us, but the Democratic party that changed, drifting steadily leftward. Thus my pleasure in reading today that George Bush was judged to have won the presidential debate last night, leaving him with his lead intact. Let's hope so.

SEPTEMBER 29th Thursday Rehearsal Day #11

Work Through 2nd Part Act II

It's been interesting to discover in China the pleasures of anonymity. Having spent most of my life with a public face, I'd forgotten what it felt like to be a private man, even in public. Celebrity has its advantages and disadvantages, of course (like just about everything else). Mostly advantages in my case, since I don't have the manic celebrity of a rock star, where you can't put your face out a door without people screaming at you. True, I could never take my kids to Disneyland (though I could get them passes). But I can move with reasonable freedom on a public street (as long as I walk fast), and I can get a table at a restaurant or tickets to a show or a seat on a plane.

Here, of course, where no American films made since World War II have been released, I'm completely anonymous . . . except in the lobby of the Great Wall Sheraton, which is filled every morning when I go to work with European and American tour groups, waiting to climb into their buses. I've found the best solution is (again) to walk very fast, so I don't turn anyone down, which is bad. I also have Mr. Li pick me up out on the street corner, beyond the hotel entrance, which also gets us off to rehearsal a little quicker, not having to fight through the tour buses.

I'm gradually closing in on the second act now. It begins with Maryk's testimony, his four separate little stories, then Queeg's monumental collapse (monumental if it works, boring if it doesn't). Then you have the two attorneys' closing statements and Greenwald's searing apostrophe in the party scene. OK, maybe not the last half of *Oedipus* or *Macbeth* on a 10-point scale of difficulty, but no piece of cake. At least a seven for toughness . . . maybe add a point for being in Chinese?

We put the Maryk stories in pretty good shape yesterday and moved in some detail through the easy part of Queeg's testimony. Once he gets those steel balls out and starts coming apart, it gets tricky, *because it can't happen all at once.* From that point, Queeg never stops speaking; he has to move in the middle of a phrase from reality to fantasy, from past to present, from easy assurance to the raw, manic edge of paranoia . . . and we have to believe him. The audience mustn't know where he's going; therefore, *he* mustn't know where he's going. I don't know of another part of this importance where the actor must just surrender himself to the scene, like a swimmer tossed in a running river. And yet (of course, always "and yet"), you have to shape what you do. Yeah . . . very tricky. Well, nobody ever said it was supposed to be easy.

God knows it's a great scene. I played it several hundred times and never got tired of it, never even got through exploring all there was in it. Captain Queeg and his steel balls have somehow earned a permanent place in the language, even with people who've never read the book, seen the play, or even the movie (where Humphrey Bogart only got to do some two minutes of this scene). How can this be? Scenes like this have a life of their own, independent of the normal process of public perception.

I haven't really touched this with Zhu Xu (who's playing the part). He's a lean actor with a serious face and large eyes; oddly enough, he looks rather like Bogart, though much taller. He doesn't really have the physical equipment to suggest the model naval officer that Queeg's Act I scene allows him to present, thus setting up the audience for the collapse in Act II. Zhu is considered one of the best actors in China, though; in the first scene, he very plausibly presents the outward image of the officer Queeg desperately wants to be.

(To paraphrase Herman Wouk, it's a question of manner and bearing.) The big challenge in the role is the Act II break-down. We'll get to that. **[All this stuff is pretty technical in here . . . like listening to an architect explain how you calculate the radii on a spiral staircase. I've found, though, that people seem interested in how you put a play together or cut a film. So I've left it in. Skip it, if it doesn't suit you.]**

I rode back through the bicycles with Mr. Li at the end of a long, really tough day, stepped out into the lobby and back into celebrity. The tour buses were unloading, with the Instamatics and little videocams grinding away as I walked to the elevator. (God curse the private videocam . . . pointed at me, at least.)

I got into an elevator with a pleasant group of Americans, one of whom praised Northwestern, where I studied acting, as she had too, she said. She's right . . . it's a fine school (also where I met Lydia). The woman's husband then said he could never decide whether he liked me better in *Elmer Gantry* or *From Here to Eternity*. I agreed it was a hard question, but I was careful not to point out that I wasn't in either film.

I learned long ago not to do that. People never believe you and it irritates them enormously; I'm not sure why. Perhaps it's partly that they think you're trying to make fun of a memory that's clear and perfect to them. I've had people describe in detail meetings we had on locations for films that were actually shot in another country from the one they recall, sometimes with other actors.

I think movies have a mythic significance for all of us. Our memories of them have a certain magic that's somehow deeply precious. When I got off at my floor, the man held the door open a moment and asked, "Didn't you win one of your Oscars for *Elmer Gantry*?"

"No, I didn't," I said. (Burt Lancaster did, of course.) "I sure wish I had, though."

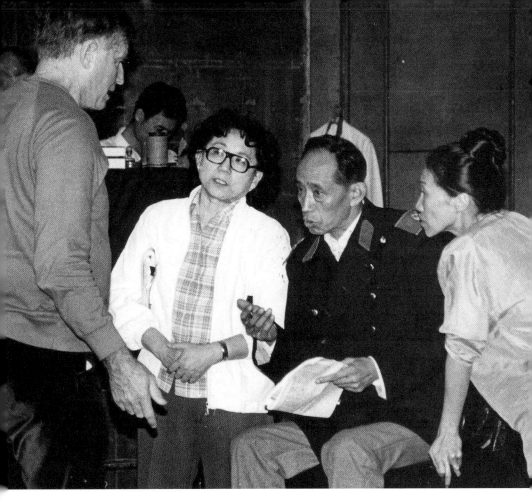

Ren Baoxian absorbing direction from Chuck while Mme. Xie prepares her astonishing "instant Mandarin." (She has translated many English-language plays into Mandarin. We later discovered she is equally fluent in French.) Though she spent six years on a pig farm making bricks during the Cultural Revolution, she lost none of her language facility. She did, however, lose her husband. We never learned any details of her experience, and we did not ask, as she would approach the subject and then conceal herself behind a bitter grin.

SEPTEMBER 30th Friday Rehearsal Day #12

We worked very hard on Act I today, with Lydia coming in to shoot it. Since all the characters appear, it's a good choice for her to cover in rehearsal. She used two cameras and did well, I thought. My girl tends toward skeptical gloom during a shoot. Certainly an underlit rehearsal hall is not ideal for photography. I remain confident.

She and Maggie joined me for lunch in my dressing room. The theatre's taken some pains to make me comfortable here and I'm grateful, though I think they've gone further than they should've. (I have a little refrigerator full of beer and soda, but the carton it came in is still out in the hall. I suspect it'll be returned when I leave.)

[I think now they were at some pains to insulate not just my beer and soda, but me, while we were in China. Given the events of last June, you can see why. To open even a crack in the walls of a totalitarian state is risky business, as the Soviets are discovering, too.]

Before we started rehearsals, they asked me what sort of schedule I wanted to go with. I said I'd accommodate to their custom, which turns out to be an hour and a half for lunch, allowing the actors a little rest after they've eaten. That's fine with me. The American system is dumb, though we'll never give it up. At home, we schedule for a firm one-hour break, on stage and in film, but by the time you've got the laggards collected and the women's hair and makeup and wardrobe checked, you're well over an hour and a quarter.

The best system is what they call "French hours," though how the French, of all people, arrived at it I'll never

Veteran actor Zhu Xu tries out a scene with Chuck. Mme. Xie looks on, and Bette Bao Lord, herself Chinese and a bulwark of the entire **Caine** *project (assistant translator, problem solver, and soother of international misapprehensions) stands by to help. Bette's superb book* **Legacies** *will be read a hundred years from now.*

understand. You start at eleven and work straight through till seven or eight with no break . . . sandwiches and whatnot on the side. The people who actually do the work love it, but you can only do it overseas. At home, the union managements won't permit it.

Anyway, the People's Art Theatre is used to an hour and a half for lunch. Some of the actors live here in the compound. The long break gives them a little downtime at lunch with their kids. That's fine with me. If we get some extra sack-time, I can do that anywhere . . . in a limo or the back of a prop truck, or, by God, in a makeup chair while they turn me into Andrew Jackson or Henry VIII at six o'clock in the damn morning. Acting . . . directing, too . . . is at least twenty percent energy. Mental focus and physical energy: You have to have it, and you have to be able to fill up the tank . . . anywhere, anytime. I do believe I can still do that.

The PAT people are sure Lord trying to help me. The first day of rehearsal, they caught me dragging a settee from the hall into my dressing room, so I could sack out in the extra time we had at lunch. My God, such consternation; you'd think they'd found me naked in the street. The next day, the settee was gone, replaced by what looked to me like a U.S. Marine Corps cot from the embassy. It's very comfortable. (So was the settee.)

There's also a good reading light and a sink. The toilet's down the hall, but that's common in theatres all over the world. I remember the first Broadway play I ever did, in remote support of Katharine Cornell in *Antony and Cleopatra.* I was dressing in a cubicle on the fourth floor of the Martin Beck Theatre, sharing a toilet down the hall with a dozen other kids, none of us rating private plumbing. One night we heard a scream from a neighboring cubicle where an actress (later famous) was dressing. We found her stark naked on the floor among the fragments of the broken sink, water flooding the room, along with her tears. A mouse had run across her foot, she'd leaped in terror to the safety of the sink, which had torn out of the wall. At this point, the old Irish stage doorman came laboring up the stairs. He wasn't impressed. "How many times I gotta tell you actresses?" he snorted. "Don't pee in the goddam sink!"

Earlier I mentioned the PAT compound. It's precisely that: an extensive walled block encompassing the theatre itself, as well as the dressing rooms, rehearsal halls, offices, scene shops, and technical support facilities. There are also some living spaces, though I've not seen them and have no idea how commodious they are. I don't know how they're allocated, either . . . there's certainly not enough room for the entire company. There are more than a hundred actors alone on the PAT roster, as well as a large technical staff. I believe the chief designer lives on the grounds; I know some actors do, with their families. I often see little kids playing in front of the scene shop when I drive in to work in the morning. (Lots of sawdust and good sticks.) Sometimes I can hear their cries, echoing through the windows as we rehearse. I like that.

Everyone in the company gets paid all the time (for life, as far as I can tell), whether they're working on a play or not, but the wages are pitifully small. Seniority seems to count, as with longshoremen and autoworkers back home. That's why the older extras in our court-martial board make more than Ren Baoxian, who plays a leading role.

There seem to be no "stars" in the Western sense, though some film actors are more widely known than others. Ying Ruocheng, for example, has an international identity from his work in *The Last Emperor,* as well as his position as Vice Minister of Culture. The Chinese have no Sly Stallones or Bette Midlers, though. Here, actors do what we all started out hoping to do . . . make a living.

We worked through the first act today, detailing here and there. I'm still worried about the timing. I clocked a few of the shorter scenes against our London times. They're playing about a minute long. Gnnarrff!!

[I've been carrying on here about the running time of the *Caine* in Chinese, because it concerned me. This is almost entirely a subjective judgment (except for getting the curtain down before the last buses leave). In the end, a scene, a play, or a movie is long when it *seems* long. I've sat through twenty-four-minute TV sitcoms that surely ran two hours, but Olivier could carry you through any of Shakespeare's longer soliloquies while you held one breath.]

Nevertheless, we worked well. It turns out we can't rehearse tomorrow . . . National Day. I understand these things, it happens all over the world. I just wish they'd *tell* me beforehand so I can schedule the time I actually have.

Ying Ruocheng was in today, to watch a piece of the first act. He felt my idea of having Urban play his ignorant young signalman with a country accent, as we did in England and the U.S., wouldn't work . . . that in China a specific rural dialect would just call attention to the fact that everyone was speaking Chinese. I don't know . . . he may be right; maybe not, but it's a hard point for me to argue. In any event, Ying has promised to retranslate all the boy's dialogue, making it simpler. This will help us.

I broke off a little early today, which gave us an hour to go through the National Art Museum. I wouldn't call it a great collection; they're obviously short of funds for maintenance and supervision. Most of the really good stuff went to Taiwan forty years ago, I expect. Still, it's always nice to walk through quiet halls and look at pictures.

Driving home through the early winter dusk in the front seat of Mr. Li's ice-blue Shanghai, I contemplated the Beijing traffic. It's not horrendous, compared to Tokyo or Mexico City, but it is total anarchy. For one thing, it's eighty percent bicycles and pedestrians. "Well," you say, "not in the street, though." Oh, yes, all over the street. They make the wildest New York jaywalkers look like Republicans. For one thing, along with the cyclists, they're convinced the stoplights are only for the cars. No kidding! I'm told there've been TV campaigns to educate the public that *everyone* is supposed to stop for a red light. Forget it. Moving smoothly down a six-lane avenue with extra bicycle paths on each side (some Beijing streets are eighty yards wide), you see green lights ahead and only five or six cars visible. Look out! At any moment, pedestrians or cyclists may loom up at you, against a red light, or out of the bushes in the middle of the block, none of them with lights, fluorescent tape, or a care in the world. I understand why Mr. Li doesn't talk much while he's driving.

Tonight, we had a change from the superb Chinese food we've been scarfing up. Antonio and Teresa Zamora (he runs the Great Wall Sheraton which is putting us up on the cuff) took us all to a very creditable Italian restaurant in another hotel. It gave us a welcome change. Good pasta and a good dry Italian white. We couldn't ask for more, and we didn't.

OCTOBER 1st Saturday No Rehearsal . . . National Day

9:00 Tennis lesson
11:30 Drive to Summer Palace
12:00 Lunch at the Listening to the Orioles Pavilion

So we couldn't rehearse today, which I didn't know till yesterday. There are all these little extra times off for the company that I don't hear about in advance. I'm not against it . . . I just want to *know* about it (grumble, grumble). I want to ease the rehearsal schedule for the actors—they're coming on very well, and I don't want them to peak too soon—but I have to know when we *can't* work. Ahh, never mind . . . I got to hit some tennis balls this morning and forgot about the play.

Then we drove out to the Summer Palace, which Lydia and Maggie saw last week. The first palace was built nearby in the 12th century, beside a small lake in what must have been a pastoral wilderness. Both lake and palace were considerably elaborated by succeeding dynasties over the next seven centuries. It's hard to describe the architectural extravagance they achieved, the fantasies they rendered: solid marble ships in the lake and sculptured hills that turn into tiny Himalayas for the eye. Versailles shrinks in comparison (though, of course, the French didn't have so much time to

On Sunday, Chuck would release the actors for a day with their families and spend his leisure time sketching the Great Wall garden. He works entirely in ink and finds this activity restorative. I personally think his ability unusually fine, but he insists on maintaining his amateur status, a luxury he does not enjoy, of course, in the theatre.

spend on theirs, what with the English and the Renaissance and All That).

Mind you, the Summer Palace was just for the hot months, when the Beijing heat is oppressive. You can almost empathize with the Red Guard's attempt to destroy it, during the barbaric atrocities of the Cultural Revolution more than two decades ago. I read recently that it was Chou En-lai who personally ordered regular army units to stop them, without checking with Mao.

He was right; it was well worth saving. No wonder Lydia and Maggie were glad to go back again. Of course, since this is a holiday, we were accompanied by a good part of the population of Beijing. I won't say it was like Times Square on New Year's Eve—I've been there—but it was pretty close. It would've ruined the day anywhere else; here it was only a minor inconvenience . . . because I was anonymous! All those thousands of faces jostling past us, but none of them knew me! They were intent on their children, their lunch, but not a thought to me except as a big foreigner with an ugly broken nose. (The Chinese have small noses and, I'm told, find mine grotesque. Never mind . . . it's gotten me a lot of parts.)

I was just part of the throng, happily ignored . . . until I sat down to sketch. I'd read that the Chinese are a naturally curious people: four minutes after I started drawing a bridge with some kids on it, while Lydia and Maggie went off with their cameras, I was surrounded by a crowd that grew to at least twenty people, watching me do a simple pen sketch. They were perfectly quiet and courteous, careful to keep my sight line open, but apparently fascinated that I should be there . . . drawing!

Actually, I don't think they cared about the drawing; it was the spectacle of a big, ugly round-eye sitting still. We found the same thing at lunch. We ate in Listening to the Orioles Pavilion—a marvelous name, especially when you try to imagine when it was simply a private place where an emperor could come and listen to orioles. There's no emperor now, and no orioles. It's a public restaurant, the only one we've eaten in outside a hotel.

They put us in a small room across a stone-floored courtyard, with only one table. There was an Oriental couple sitting there; we were given seats across from them. There were no other patrons in the room, but waiters kept peering in at us from the doorway. We were curiosities. We enjoyed what I suppose was a real Chinese restaurant meal, intent on absorbing the feel of the place, as much as the food. There were intricately carved columns encrusted with dragons some centuries old embedded in a plain concrete floor, clearly laid only a few years ago.

After some time, the other couple spoke shyly to me, in careful, halting English. Of course, they weren't Chinese at all, but Japanese, exiled to the private room with us, as foreigners. To them I was not anonymous. We communicated inadequately . . . I kept drawing little pictures, which gets the idea across, but of course there had to be autographs, which I don't mind, and those damned little instant cameras, which I do. When I think of the millions of lousy photographs of me that lie curling in bureau drawers all over the world. . . . Never mind; the Summer Palace was worth it. We had a memorable day.

This is where the Dowager Empress of China, the last woman in the world to hold total political power, fled when the siege of the foreign embassies in Peking by her Boxer rebels was broken. We didn't get into this part of the story in the film (55 Days at Peking) I made about it . . . we ended with the defeat of the Boxers. I researched it, though; it's eerie to move inside this vast imperial fantasy where she lurked through her last days. Walking beside the misty lakes along the miles (yes, miles!) of roofed and stepped and balustraded walkways, every foot painted with charming and meticulous decoration, it's easy to imagine the Empress here, borne swaying in a litter back and forth in seething exile, locked in this fairy kingdom while the 20th century lurched alive twenty miles away in Peking. She was a monstrous woman . . . I remember that.

OCTOBER 2nd Sunday Day Off

10:00 Rainish morning: scrub both my tennis lesson and the picnic in the Fragrant Hills
12:00 Pat Corcoran's for lunch
2:00 Antique market for porcelains

Today had its frustrations, but turned out better in the middle. The weather and the days are drawing in together as we reach October. When we get back home, it'll be dark before dinner. I don't know why that always saddens me a little . . . because I get up at six, probably. In the winter, I chase the diminishing daylight on my ridge. We've been here just over two weeks, but the summer warmth is gone now. You can smell autumn and black coal smoke in the Beijing air.

To begin with, it rained this morning, scrubbing not only my tennis, but the picnic Pat Corcoran had planned for us with some of the embassy people in the Fragrant Hills. The Chinese have a genius for intricately exotic names . . . Inn of the Sixth Happiness, the Forbidden City, the Death of a Thousand Cuts, the Listening to the Orioles Pavilion. Still, like Stephen Vincent Benét, I love American names . . .

> *. . . The sharp names that never get fat,*
> *The snakeskin-titles of mining-claims,*
> *The plumed war-bonnet of Medicine Hat,*
> *Tucson and Deadwood and Lost Mule Flat . . .*

> *I will remember Carquinez Straits,*
> *Little French Lick and Lundy's Lane,*
> *The Yankee ships and the Yankee dates*
> *And the bullet-towns of Calamity Jane.*
> *I will remember Skunktown Plain. . . .*

I shall not rest quiet in Montparnasse.
I shall not lie easy at Winchelsea.
You may bury my body in Sussex grass,
You may bury my tongue at Champmédy.
I shall not be there. I shall rise and pass.
Bury my heart at Wounded Knee.

All this by way of saying we didn't *get* to picnic in the Fragrant Hills, but lunched very comfortably in Pat and Renata Corcoran's flat. We drove afterward to the flea market, where Pat guided Lydia and Maggie to some useful antique buys, minus the five hundred percent markup in the hotel shops. I spent much of the time sketching, but it was a pleasure to watch Pat's good-humored bargaining in fluent Mandarin. His wife said a good thing: "It's not just that he speaks Chinese so well. It's that he *likes* them and they know that."

We came back to the hotel midafternoon; I was looking forward to an easy session ruminating on the last week on Igor, the portable son of Aggie, my computer back home. The crafty thug broke down again (or betrayed me, or just surrendered, like the black-hearted, lick-spittle dog I've suspected he was all along). Kevin, the hotel computer expert, came up and wrestled for an hour, accompanied by two impassive Chinese trainees. Three long overseas calls to Mark McIntire, my computer guru in Los Angeles (yes, you *need* a guru!) got us nowhere. For the time being, I'm reduced to this old IBM electric they loaned me. The more I become dependent on computers, the more disturbed I am by their malevolent personae. Almost all of them are female, mind you, making them all the more inscrutable to us beleaguered males.

OCTOBER 3rd Monday Rehearsal Day #13

9:30 PAT rehearse Act II
5:30 Pat Corcoran's aptmnt . . . calligraphers' meeting

In terms of performance, the company's moving well toward where I want them to be in two weeks. Not yet. That's why I moved the rehearsal call back half an hour today. We have to come up to speed in their time and my time and the play's time.

Time. Yes, it's still a problem as rehearsal brings us nearer to where we should be. Oddly, the short scenes play in Mandarin pretty much the same as in English. But the more complex ideas explored in some of the speeches simply take longer to say in Chinese. Aside from what this does to the overall running time, it distorts the internal tempo of the scenes as well. We may have to make further cuts. Christ, why didn't I study Chinese?!

The performances are also ripening at different rates, which is OK. The actors are variously gifted and experienced, the parts are variously complicated. They're all up for this play; it's up to me to make them come together at the same time.

Tonight, we went to the Corcorans for dinner and had a fascinating exposure to the work of some half-dozen Chinese calligraphers Pat had invited over to meet me, each expert in a different style. I'd first studied calligraphy just because my handwriting was so lousy, but it was interesting to see masters at work. I even managed to avoid total embarrassment, trying the brush myself, only because I'm a fair graphic mimic. It wasn't clear to me whether the eight men were amateurs, revered for their mastery of the art but mak-

One wonderful evening Pat Corcoran invited a number of his Chinese calligrapher friends to dinner. Afterward, they demonstrated their artistry. Chuck, with his draftsman's skills, was enthralled. We brought back several fascinating examples from different periods of Chinese lettering, elegant in their casual swirls and blots.

ing a living in other fields, or men whose skills alone earned them a place in the hierarchy. I hope the latter is true. What they can do with a brush is awesome.

OCTOBER 4th Tuesday Rehearsal Day #14
(also my birthday)

9:30 PAT rehearse Act I
12:00 Birthday lunch . . . only halfway through Keith scene
1:00 till 3:00 Actors' seminar—wrap for day at 3:00
7:30 LV for Maxim's w/Lydia, Maggie: her b'day present (also w/Lords)

There was a hell of a lot of birthday in this one. It started with a cake in the front door at 6:30 AM from all our people back in Coldwater, along with my breakfast. I took this to the theatre to share with the actors.

[Looking back, I'm not sure whether the Chinese do birthday cakes. Birthday celebrations, certainly, but a cake with candles may have been new to my company. In any case, they were most vociferous in ushering me into another year. Actors and athletes celebrate very well.]

The cake consumed, we got in a couple of hours of actual rehearsal on Act I. The cast had organized a birthday lunch, with an even larger cake **[no candles . . . that may be a Western detail].** Ying Ruocheng appeared, with several other distinguished figures from the Chinese theatre. Then we had entertainment by some of the actors (Yang Lixin, who plays Lieutenant Bird, the condescending young psychiatrist, at least as good in his part as either of two other actors I've directed) gave a marvelous falsetto performance as a French maid in a spoof of French farce. This all ran until lunch, when Lydia and Maggie joined us, followed by a seminar the cast requested, me talking about so forth and so forth. (I had to be careful to reminisce about work they had at least heard of. It's surprising that they trust me, when you think of it. None of my films has ever been shown commercially in China, only in private embassy screenings.)

By the end of the seminar, there was nothing to do but give the company the rest of the day off. This evening, Maggie, as her gift, took us all to Maxim's, now decorated in elaborate fin de siècle style. Ambassador Lord and Bette joined us. All in all, it was one of the most thoroughly celebrated birthdays I can recall. I confess myself touched (and we *did* rehearse for two hours).

On Chuck's birthday (October 4), Bette Bao Lord and members of the cast and theatre staff threw a huge and delightful party in his honor, a surprise that stunned him with pleasure. My most vivid memory: a song from the Long March of '49. Even my anti-Communist husband felt the hair rise on the back of his neck.

OCTOBER 5th Wednesday Rehearsal Day #15

7:30 Shoot TV interview footage around hotel
9:00 PAT, call
9:30 2nd half Keith scene
11:40 Finish Act I, shoot TV footage Queeg scene
12:00 Act II wrap, lunch
1:15 Film TV Interview
1:30 Act II
3:45 Finish Act II
4:15 Hotel

We finished Act I, did all of Act II, today . . . a little more than what we've done in a day so far. Some of the performances are rounding into shape well: Ren Baoxian's Lieutenant Greenwald, certainly (and most importantly). Southard and Bird are fine, Lundeen and Urban soon will be. At this point, Gu Wei is OK as Captain Blakely, the presiding judge. Xiu Zongdi is maybe a little better than that as Lieutenant Keefer, the weak-souled manipulator who's really precipitated the mutiny. So is Cong Lin as Lieutenant Keith, the green young reserve officer caught in the middle. I'm worried about Wu Guiling as Commander Challee, the able, decent prosecutor that Greenwald blindsides to win the case, and about Xiao Peng as Lieutenant Maryk, the defendant. Neither actor is ideally cast physically, neither is moving very fast toward understanding his part . . . or doing it, anyway. Yet. That's OK . . . there's time.

Zhu Xu will find his way, I think, but he has a lot further to go . . . it's a very tough part. I really don't know yet how to direct him in the breakdown scene . . . it's such a basket of snakes. I have to help him find his Queeg without imposing mine. I will. He'll come to it.

[An actor, directing, has a special problem: You tend to point the actor toward what you'd do yourself . . . particularly if you've actually played the part. You have to communicate what you want as a director without making the actor give your performance. A slippery business.]

OCTOBER 6th Thursday Rehearsal Day #16

5:00 U.S. Embassy, meet staff: photo op, autographs, etc. TV in-terviews, dinner

My anxieties about both the performances and the timing were eased by our run-through of both acts today. We're now only seven or eight minutes longer than when it played in England. I think I can accept that, given the tonal complexities of the Chinese language. Challee and Maryk were both better today, particularly Challee. I still have a long way to go with Queeg and Greenwald, but both parts are much harder and both actors have larger talents.

We had a curious little crisis today. I resolved it easily enough, but I learned a little about the Chinese and a lot about Communist bureaucracy in the process. There are about a hundred actors permanently employed in this company, on a demeaningly small yearly salary, with some of them getting living quarters in the compound as well. When they are actually performing in a play, there is an additional stipend, its size depending solely on the actor's seniority in the company. When *Caine Mutiny* opens, some of the older actors cast as members of the court, who never speak, will be paid more than the actors playing the leading roles.

Last week, I found out that an additional stipend is paid to actors who are rehearsing . . . a flat fifty cents a day. This seemed to me such a revoltingly tiny sum that I felt driven to do something about it. I called Bette Bao Lord at the embassy and made her understand how strongly I felt. It's well enough for me to work free: I can afford it, and they can't afford to pay me. But to rehearse eight hours a day for fifty cents? I told Bette I'd like to contribute a few hundred dollars to flesh out our company's rehearsal compensation. She said she'd like to join me, but pointed out that the actors would be compelled to throw the money into a common pot, to share with everyone else in the People's Art Theatre.

"I won't do that, Bette," I said. "I don't believe in that. I want to get the money in the pockets of the people who are doing the work: the actors, the assistants, the interpreters who are helping us raise *Caine*." Bette agreed and undertook to go to Ying Ruocheng at the Ministry of Culture. He agreed, too, which bore a little more weight, and we gave the money, shared among only the *Caine* company. A done deal.

Not quite. This morning, as always, I was in the rehearsal room well before nine. Given the language barrier, I can't be part of the usual actors' morning banter. We greet each other in Mandarin (I can do that, but I don't want to put Mme. Xie to work before I have to). I read the *Herald Tribune* for ten minutes, then discussed the scenes I wanted to work on with Ren Ming, my assistant. At ten of nine, I got the actors' attention and announced the work schedule for the day, then sat down to finish my tea before the hour ticked over. I suddenly noticed an odd little man in a double-breasted suit and a blue tam standing in the center of the room addressing the company . . . in Mandarin, of course. I leaned over and asked Mme. Xie what he was saying.

She listened a moment. "More or less what you just told the actors," she said.

I got the pitch. I walked to the center of the room and said, "I don't know what the custom is in China, but in America no one gives instructions to the actors but the director. When this man has left our rehearsal, we will begin. I don't want to see him in this theatre again."

It turns out he had been an executive here during the shambles of the Cultural Revolution, when the current and previous head of the theatre had been banished to shoveling coal. The little man in the tam had hung on in a minor clerical position, and thought to join the company and thus earn the rehearsal bonus, too.

I have no illusions, of course. He won't set foot in the compound while we're working here, but once the big ugly round-eye has gone, he'll be back, doing whatever it is he does. Full employment . . . among the joys of the socialist state.

OCTOBER 7th Friday Rehearsal Day #17

9:30 PAT run Act I
11:00 Notes to cast
12:00 Lunch
1:30 Run whole play for crew
7:00 Dinner w/Maggie, Zamoras, Justine's

I'm back in Igor's brain again, sneaky bastard that he is. But I need him, and Mark McIntire had sent out another floppy disk with the program I'm using. Kevin King, Mark's Kiwi counterpart here, put it in for me, and we're in shape again. I feel like an idiot to be so incompetent in this crucial capacity ("technopeasant," my son calls it), but as Will Rogers pointed out memorably, "We're all of us ignorant . . . just on different subjects."

We worked on the first act this morning, bits-and-piecing, then after lunch did a run-through of the whole play with a pickup audience of a couple of dozen people from the technical staff. I was relieved to discover that the few comic bits—Urban, some of the other scenes—work for a Chinese audience. Of course, they applauded at the end. Of course.

I drove home brooding about the way the play's going and once again watching, in bemused fascination, the Beijing traffic. There are very few cars, almost none of them private. The streets are packed with pedestrians and bicyclists, who set the pace and, frankly, terrify me. My driver, Mr. Li, seems perfectly serene, threading his way sedately through a torrent of humanity, unaware, or uncaring, of their own fragile vulnerability. A New York cabbie would go crazy here. On the major six-lane streets, there are people on bicycles on every lane divider, weaving back and forth.

Chuck demonstrating Captain Queeg's final breakdown, when his sense of what he is and what he is trying to say in his defense utterly deserts him, filling him with uncontrollable anger at his ship's company. After the last rehearsals Zhu Xu grasped the elements of the scene and gave a shattering performance as Queeg.

Even when you find yourself on a side avenue with no traffic at all in sight and green lights ahead, you daren't speed up; at any moment, a fragile matriarch may plunge out in the middle of a darkened block. A bicyclist with a four-year-old on the handle bars will pedal firmly across in front of you. They used to say Orientals don't value human life that much. I don't believe that. Every man values his own life, and his child's. I think a lot of people in the streets here simply don't realize how lethal motor vehicles are, even at twenty miles an hour.

We had a pleasant dinner with the Zamoras. (The Sheraton people have really been crucial in this undertaking, and this was Maggie Field's last night with us). Back in the hotel, I talked to Lydia about how to communicate to Zhu Xu (my Queeg) my understanding of the complexities of his breakdown. As usual, her advice was sound, but I'm still not comfortable with where we are with that part. I fell asleep in my chair, reading through the scene.

OCTOBER 8th Saturday Rehearsal Day #18

9:30 PAT work on bits of Act II
10:30 Notes etc.
1:30 Run play through 1st half of Queeg scene, Act II
4:15 Break, no notes
6:00 Maggie to airport w/Lydia. We have quiet evening in suite.

I'd planned to run through the whole play from the top this afternoon (with another small group of theatre staff as audience). I cut it short just before Queeg's breakdown. Some of the actors had a performance tonight, but I didn't really want Zhu Xu to do that scene today anyway.

I'd better fill you in a little on this scene. Captain Queeg appears in Act I, the first witness to testify. He comes across as the model naval commander he wants so much to be. An audience unfamiliar with Wouk's novel should be persuaded that Queeg is right, that Lieutenant Maryk was guilty of mutiny, though the testimony through the rest of Act I puts this in some doubt.

In the second act, Queeg is called again, to be cross-examined by Lieutenant Greenwald, who is defending Maryk. At first, Queeg's testimony is still cool, relaxed, and eminently plausible. But under Greenwald's skilled and increasingly relentless interrogation, his composure trembles, then cracks. At last, in response to Greenwald's question about the log Maryk had kept on Queeg's irrational behavior, Queeg launches on an impassioned monologue that takes him further and further from reality. In the end, he's no longer in the courtroom, nor talking to anyone there, but to a changing group of men he remembers, from the *Caine* to his service as a young ensign twenty years before, scraping the bare bone of his troubled psyche. Maryk is undeniably vindicated. Queeg walks out of the court with his career in ruins.

I know of no other single speech in any play I'm familiar with that so effectively alters what the audience feels, or so radically resolves the play itself. Here it is:

GREENWALD

Commander Queeg, have you read Lieutenant Maryk's medical log?

QUEEG

Yes, I have read that interesting document, yes, sir, indeed I have. It's the biggest conglomeration of lies and distortions and half-truths I've ever seen. But I'm extremely glad you asked me about it because I want to get the truth about all this on the record. The whole *truth.*

GREENWALD

Please state your version, or any factual comments on the episodes in the log, sir.

QUEEG

'Kay. Now, starting right with that strawberry business? The real truth is that I was betrayed and thrown and double-crossed by my executive officer and this precious gentleman, Mister Keith. Between them they corrupted my wardroom so I was one man against the whole ship, without any support from my officers. 'Kay. Now, you take that strawberry business. Why, if that wasn't a clear-cut case of conspiracy to protect a malefactor from justice . . . ? Maryk carefully leaves out the little fact that I had conclusively proved by a process of elimination that someone had a key to the icebox. He says it was the steward's mates who ate the strawberries?! [He laughs] If I wanted to take the trouble, I could prove to this court GEOMETRICALLY that they couldn't have.

[Abruptly, he turns to the judge, who looks a little baffled.] *It's the water business all over again! When the crew was taking showers seven times a* day!! [To Maryk, now] *Our evaporators were definitely on the fritz, hah?* [Maryk nods] *'Kay! Half the time!* [Triumphant, now] *I was trying to inculcate the simplest PRINCIPLES of water conservation, but no . . . Mr. Maryk, the hero of the crew, wanted to go right on mollycoddling them! You take that coffee . . .* [A small pause now, he takes the steel balls from his pocket.] *No . . . No . . . the strawberry thing first.* [He turns to the court again.] *It all hinged on a thorough search for the KEY, and that is where Mr. Maryk, as usual with the help of Mr. Keith, completely fudged it!* [To Maryk again] *You just went through a whole lot of phony motions that proved NOTHING! Like the incessant burning out of those coffee silexes . . .* which were government property! [To court] *They took it as a joke . . . every one of them, from Maryk on down. No SENSE of responsibility, though I emphasized over and over: The war will NOT last* forever. *Two more years? . . . five years? . . . sooner or later all these things will* have *to be* accounted for. [To Challee, now] *It was a constant battle . . . always the same thing: Maryk and Keith undermining my authority, always an argument . . . though I personally . . . I liked Keith . . . very much. I kept trying to train him up . . . only to be stabbed in the back . . . wh . . .* [His voice breaks.] *'Kay. I believe that covers the . . . uh . . . strawberry thing.* [To court, suddenly revived] *Oh, yes, the wardroom mess accounts! I had to watch THEM like a hawk . . . and believe me, I did. They didn't slip any fast ones by ME, but it was NOT for lack of trying!* [To Maryk now, who seems daunted by Queeg's passion. From the beginning, Greenwald has been sitting on the edge of his desk, arms folded in quiet respect.] *No, instead of paying some attention to your accounts and your inventories, which I had to check over and over.* [To Challee] *Always, a few pennies short . . . a few dollars over. What did it matter to them, keeping accurate records? Let the Captain worry. And I did, by GOD. I defy anyone to check over a single wardroom mess* statement or ship's service inventory filed aboard the USS CAINE while I was captain and find a mistake of one single solitary CENT!! [A small pause] 'Kay . . . what else. There was so much TRIPE in that precious log of Mr. Maryk's [Turns to Maryk] Ah . . . the movie business?? 'Kay. [To court] No respect for command . . . that was the whole trouble aboard that ship!! . . . And the movie projectionist. [There's the projectionist, suddenly, in front of him] He's got a surly, disrespectful manner, anyway. Starting the movie without waiting for the arrival of the commanding officer?! Yeah, and out of this whole ship's company, officers and men, did one man call a halt . . . or even notice that the captain was not PRESENT? I missed those movies, too . . . as much as they did . . . but I banned them and by God I'd do it again! What did they expect me to do, hand out letters of commendation to everybody for this BLATANT INSULT to the commanding officer?! It's not . . . NOT that I take it personally. It's the PRINCIPLE . . . the principle of respect for COMMAND! That principle was DEAD when I came aboard this ship . . . and I nagged and I crabbed and I bitched and I hollered, but I brought it back to LIFE . . . and I'll make it stick too, by God, so long as I'm captain. [Suddenly, quietly, to the yeoman-stenotypist who's recording his testimony] Sailor, you take those silexes . . . [He's back on the CAINE, easy and fatherly.] It isn't just the silex. It's a matter of respect. [Almost jocular, now] When I ask you a question, sailor, I want a straight answer. You can just knock off that shifty evasion . . . or you will be goddamn sorry! [A frenzied scream] WHAT DO I CARE FOR STRAWBERRIES!!? It's a matter of principle . . . pilfering is pilfering and on MY SHIP . . . [He's somewhere else, now, talking easily to a crony.] Not that we get so many treats, either, with that slow motion mess treasurer of ours. [He listens, with a warm chuckle.] No-o-o! It wasn't like that when I was an ensign, believe you me. They made ME jump, sure enough. [Salutes . . . suddenly, he IS an ensign.] Aye, aye, SIR! [Another shift] And when we do get something pleasant, like strawberries, once in a blue moon . . . if

I can't have more when I feel like it . . . that's an outrage. No sir. They are not gonna get away with that. There will be no more of it, BY GOD! NOT ON MY SHIP!! [This is shouted to Challee, whose calming hand gesture brings him suddenly back to the courtroom.] *Where was I?* [He turns and points to the yeoman-stenotypist.] *Yeoman! How many of these things have I covered?* [Yeoman, scared, looks at Blakely, who shakes his head. Queeg turns to him, his shaking hand stilled with an effort.] *I can only do this roughly, from MEMORY.* [He sees he still holds the steel balls, pockets them, turning to Greenwald.] *You ask me specific questions. I'll tackle 'em, one by one.* [A desperate death's head grin]

It's the key scene in the play. Film buffs still remember the fragment of it Bogart did in the film version. The full scene is very complex, both technically and emotionally, like doing a triple off the high board and finishing a couple of bars of *Aida* before you hit the water. The whole business with the steel balls has to be worked out: when you get them out, what you do with them so the audience sees them when you want them to as well as how . . . which hand at which point and so forth (also for God's sake don't drop one).

[I did, once, on tour in Brighton before the London opening, where I acted Queeg as well as directing. I'd warned the actors against this dread possibility. "Above all," I said, "do not pick it up." No one did. The ball rolled several feet and stopped just before falling into the audience. *That* would have been a disaster. Actually it worked quite well as a silent moment in Queeg's collapse. I don't recommend trying to stage it that way.]

It's a soliloquy, really; about eight minutes, which is longer than any in Shakespeare, though not nearly so daunting a man-killer as those monsters, of course. (Still, the steel balls are a complication . . . like doing the duel in *Hamlet* and "To be or not to be . . ." at the same time.)

I don't know anything in acting as exciting . . . as releasing . . . as one of these *mano a manos.* Just you and the text. When it happens, it's like an orgasm. I remember it working for me a few times doing Tom's narration in Williams's *Glass Menagerie* and the long reminiscence O'Neill gives his old actor in *Long Day's Journey,* as well as, more rarely, some of the major Shakespeare mountains. *(Those mothers will bring you to your knees just about every time.)*

Queeg's rambling, chaotic testimony, like the dagger soliloquy in *Macbeth,* is largely hallucinatory . . . a kaleidoscope of past and present, changing time and place in the middle of a sentence. We discussed it in some detail, exploring a way through it. We have some time yet, but he has a good way to go. He has to surrender himself to the scene first.

I got back to the hotel a little washed out myself, just in time to say goodbye to Maggie before she left for the airport with Lydia. It was marvelous to have her with us.

OCTOBER 9th Sunday Day Off

8:30 Paperwork
11:00 Tennis lesson
7:00 Szechuan restaurant w/Lydia, J. Doolittle, Bette Lord, Tina
   Chen

One of the nice things about working hard is that you value more the time when you're *not* working . . . it really *counts*. I confess I wish I were spending this Sunday on my ridge. Then I could really return fresh tomorrow to the challenge of the play and this vast, inscrutable, maybe unknowable land. **[In retrospect, given the convulsions of the last months, perhaps China *is* unknowable. In two months, I don't pretend to have an answer to that.]**

I did get some rest and a tennis hit with a sturdy, beaming Burmese pro with a vicious topspin and good English (though he greets every deep shot I hit with an enthusiastic *"Thankyew!"* Maybe because he doesn't have to come in on a short ball).

The language barrier is part of my vague feeling of difference, I'm sure. I struggle with it eight hours a day at rehearsal, lobbing messages over the wall like notes wrapped around stones, tunneling through it by acting in English while they respond in Mandarin. I've discovered one of my assistant stage managers speaks a little Spanish. (None of my actors has any more English than the fragments of Chinese I offer like flags on a foreign hill.) Her name is Carmen. (She must have some Spanish blood.) We exchange brisk Castilian phrases now and then, which I find somehow comforting, though my fluency in that language is not too great either.

They're celebrating Oktoberfest in the Sheraton, perhaps a little uncertainly, though they have leather-shorted brass bandsmen playing the appropriate songs **[No, not Chinese tuba players in lederhosen. This was a no-kidding German band.]** and wienerschnitzel and sauerkraut (more or less) on the lunch menu. Lydia and I tried it, then went out in the large gardens behind the hotel where she photographed the ducks and I sketched the tile roofs on the little whadyacallems . . . pagodas are Japanese, aren't they? Then we rested for a while. That was lovely. No language barrier there.

We ate Szechuan (God, I have to learn how to spell that) tonight on the roof, twenty-one stories up. None of the Manchu emperors, Lords of the Middle Kingdom, ever saw Beijing from so high . . . while they lived, at least. Tina Chen, who worked with me in *Hawaiians*, was with us. She was the best thing in that film, I remember.

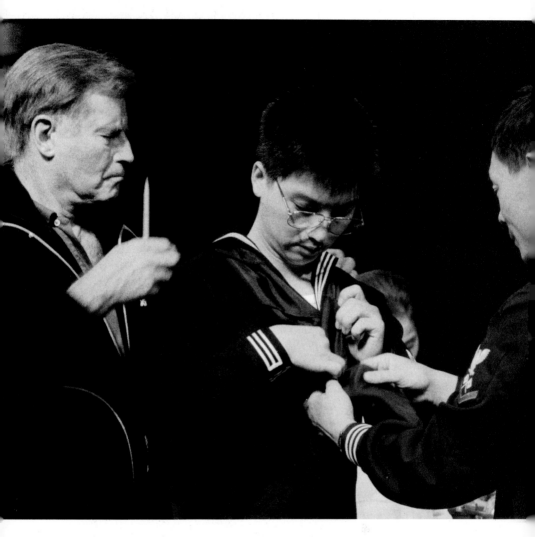

The cast members in their American naval uniforms for the first time. Chuck was intent on the accuracy of details like proper ties, and on dress rehearsal night I was amazed—our actors were transformed! It was not a superficial change but something that emerged from a depth of understanding of another philosophy, another dream. We were proud of them.

106

OCTOBER 10th Monday Rehearsal Day #19

9:30 Notes
10:00 CBS filming
1:30 Run play
2:00 Adm. Trost, CNO, to watch
4:10 Finish
7:00 W/Lydia to PAT to see Number One Restaurant

We're three six-day working weeks into this; I never expected to be this far now, this good. My assistant director, Ren Ming, deserves a lot of credit, the actors deserve more. I think I know how to motivate a cast and lead them in useful directions. Still, the sum of it is that the company's ready to move on stage, and the stage still has another play on it. I have to find things for them to do before we come around the clubhouse turn, into the stretch.

CBS was there today, filming rehearsal for a documentary they plan. (We've suddenly become media darlings . . . probably not what would've happened if I'd been asked to do this in Taiwan.) I must try to get a look at their footage. I've never had a chance to see myself directing. I might find something useful . . . film is a marvelous learning tool.

Admiral Trost, U.S. Chief of Naval Operations, here on a state visit, also dropped by, obviously interested in a play about the U.S. Navy done in Mandarin by Chinese actors. (He'd also seen me in the play in Washington.) He watched a scene rehearse, then I checked some of the actors in proper U.S.N. dress blues for the first time, with the correct WW II ribbons. The admiral was impressed; so was I. The uniforms somehow took them the last step to melting into American Navy men. I've been working with them for weeks, supervised their haircuts, the way they walk, come to attention, comport themselves in court. Now, suddenly, I see them in the uniforms and they're Navy. The metamorphosis is complete.

God knows it was trouble enough to get the uniforms right. At first, they'd planned to build them from scratch, here in Beijing. This was a disaster. The Chinese, for whatever reason, simply can't *do* uniforms. Even their armed forces have terrible uniforms.

OK, I thought . . . maybe the Navy can help me. No dice. The U.S. military is prohibited by law from donating, loaning, or selling anything to anybody, including uniforms. (Also F-14s, no doubt.) Bette Bao Lord saved us by finding an anonymous American donor who simply paid to have the uniforms made by a costume house at home.

We explored my Saturday notes in the morning, playing through various fragments, often with me doing bits in English to their Chinese, which seems an increasingly productive method. It lets me communicate more personally than I can through the extraordinary Mme. Xie, and yet insulates them from any possibility of copying my reading of the lines. (My God, when I was studying directing, what heresy that would've been!)

In the afternoon, we ran the play, which now is rounding into the right tempo. Many of the performances are very good, most of them about as good as they're going to get. Some of the extras are going a little slack . . . it's pretty boring to sit there with your back to the audience for two hours, pretending to operate a stenotype machine. I can jack them up.

I'm still worried about Queeg. Zhu's got the first scene very well; he's totally plausible as the model officer Queeg wants to be, has persuaded himself he is. But the second act breakdown daunts him, and I don't wonder: It's one mean bitch of a scene. (Ah, but what a sweet, seductive, never-mind-the-cost, let's *do* it bitch she is.)

Chuck playing Queeg, with Ren Baoxian ready to pounce for the kill.

He has to let go. I think he can, but he won't. Not so far. I've laid out the stuff with the steel balls, which is crucial, but simply technical. You learn it stone cold, like driving a chariot, or the *Macbeth* combats. But with those, you just concentrate on the mechanics, so no one gets hurt. Here, there's also the scene to play. You have to drive Queeg to his end.

You also have to be careful when an actor's having trouble with a scene. You must help him find it, but you mustn't break his belief in himself. (I remember when Willy Wyler took me aside some two weeks into the *Ben-Hur* shoot and said, "Chuck, you have to be better in this part." "Fine, Willy," I said, sucking in my gut. "Tell me how." "I can't," he said. "I don't know. If I did, I'd tell you. But you have to be better.")

That was tough. Very tough. I have a thick Scot's skin, though, which helped me. Maybe Willy knew that. I *was* better, somehow.

I can't do that with Zhu. An odd thing happened while we were working on the scene. You have to be careful in rehearsal to direct your actors as privately as you can, especially when you're asking them to explore very intimate emotions. I went to where Zhu was sitting in the witness chair and knelt beside him to make a point. There was a sudden, very audible gasp from every Chinese in the room. Zhu stood up, distressed. Mme. Xie explained to me afterward that I was surrendering face as the director by kneeling to an actor. There are cultural complications here.

Finally, I just acted the scene for him. Not to copy it; he mustn't do that, and he can't anyway . . . he doesn't know what I'm saying. But he can see the wild swings of fear and desperate invention that carry through to Queeg's collapse. The chances Queeg's driven to take in his derangement are the chances Zhu has to take as an actor, too.

Tonight Lydia and I went, on its closing night, to see the play we're following on the PAT stage: *Number One Res-*

taurant. Even with Mme. Xie translating in whispers, it was hard to follow, of course, but I wanted to see the kind of work they do. Some of my *Caine* actors were in it. It was an interesting story of Beijing in the thirties, done in a somewhat more presentational style than we're trying for with *Caine* (which is why they brought me out here, no doubt). Still, they're good actors, the more so that they can so readily pick up a more realistic method. We were impressed.

OCTOBER 11th Tuesday Rehearsal Day #20

9:30 PAT run Act I
1:30 Run Act II (not Queeg)
3:00 Break early
7:00 W/Lydia, J. Doolittle see Edberg/Agassi Tennis exhibition

The days are getting fuller, the blood's beginning to rise in the company. It mustn't come to a head yet. I didn't want to run Zhu Xu through that Act II breakdown again today, so I skipped the end of the play and let the cast go home a bit early. They're coming along about right. It's time to move out of the rehearsal room and onto the set, but they won't have it ready for tomorrow. (I've no idea why and there's no point in arguing about it.) They did get the sets from *Number One Restaurant* struck and my set on stage. It's a very plausible re-creation of the London set, rendered impressionistically, because they couldn't afford to do more. It's fine. They did a good job of following the notes and sketches I mailed in July and our discussions in the scene shop since I've been here. There was vast relief from the crew and technical staff when I checked it all out. I gather they were filled with foreboding, expecting some outburst of disapproval. Apparently, Arthur Miller was not happy with the *Salesman* set when he saw it.

Of course, once a set's built and onstage, there's not a hell of a lot you can do about it. A playwright can rewrite a scene in the morning and it'll be rehearsed in the afternoon and in performance that night. If you want to change the set, you'd better communicate that to the guys who build it before they put it on stage. *Well* before.

We went to see Edberg and Agassi play an exhibition

match tonight in a huge hall obviously designed for another sport. Whoever laid the court out didn't understand that the best place to see a tennis match is from either end of the court. The fifty-yard line is for football. They had no seats at *all* on the ends. Our seats were up in the outfield bleachers (to shift sports again). I had a little confrontation with the seating official (clearly a former Red Guard). My face is no passport here, of course, where I'm anonymous, so that didn't help, nor did the language barrier.

Still, I certainly understood him when he said, "These are your seats. Shut up and sit down!" poking me in the chest with his finger.

I gripped his wrist and said (evenly, I hope), "Don't do that." I think he understood me, too. Language is not the only communication. At this point, one of the embassy people came and cleared it up with a paragraph or two of fluent Mandarin, and we got the seats changed. If the Gang of Four were still in power, I might've had a lot more than my seat changed.

The tennis was marvelous. Edberg, just off a plane from Switzerland, was maybe a little flat (he was missing his first serve), but his deep, low slice shots were amazing. I can see why he beat Becker at Wimbledon. Agassi, whom I'd never seen in person, is remarkable . . . incredible speed, power, and court coverage. He can be a dominating player for a long time, I think. The evening gave me a nice break from the *Caine.*

OCTOBER 12th Wednesday Rehearsal Day #21

Last day in rehearsal hall
10:00 Late call PAT
10:30 Notes first act
11:00 Run first act
12:00 Lunch
1:00 Int. w/UP bureau chief
1:30 Run Act II
3:30 Notes/break
5:00 Int. w/French writer

I spent the day on a run-through, with some overall notes (some of them pretty picky, of course). You have to make the actors understand you're *watching* them. Most of the principal parts are in very good shape now. Greenwald, certainly. He needs some work on the drunk scene . . . otherwise he could open tomorrow. Bird is fine (in a much shorter, very showy part). I took a little time to sandpaper some corners there. A lot of that part is timing; that's hard to convey in another language, especially if the director doesn't know the language, syllable for syllable . . . a lot of reactions play a half-beat off the syllable. You don't *think* of it that way . . . you just do it, like Jack Benny or Mort Sahl. But how do you tell them, or even *show* them, if you don't know the beats in the other language? (Well, hell . . . as well as you can, of course. That's what I'm *doing* here . . . as well as I can.)

Challee is vastly improved as the prosecuting attorney. Aside from some sloppy physical moves, I'm happy with him. The judge, Blakely, certainly; most of the witnesses as

Wu Guiling as Challee, trying desperately to defend Captain Queeg but aware, finally, that his prosecution of Maryk is quite hopeless.

well. Maryk is heavy-handed still; he tends to overcorrect to direction. "I told you Maryk's a tough and capable man," I said to him. "He resents his situation, he's anxious about being court-martialed. That doesn't mean I want you to play him like a cornered gangster." I've been told more than once that Chinese actors like firm and specific direction. So do most actors . . . anywhere. The trick is to avoid being harsh and wrong. I'm sure I'm not harsh . . . I'm working on wrong.

Tomorrow, we move onstage; this is our last day in the rehearsal hall. I've spent a lot of my working life in them. I'll grant they're better than coal mines. (My grandfather, who started working in a mine when he was nine, made that clear to me.) Not one hell of a lot better, though. The church basement in Soho where I directed the London production of this play was just about as cold and dank as any mine I've seen. (We also rehearsed the L.A. production in a church, come to think of it, though it was a lot sunnier.) If rehearsals counted, actors would get high marks for church attendance.

We also spend more time in banquet halls than we do going to banquets. (You've no idea how drab a banquet room looks in the daytime.) Anyplace that isn't used much on weekdays is good. I say "good," meaning adequate. Most of these rooms are ugly and only barely functional for rehearsal. Dance studios are terrible: all mirrors and tall windows; the dialogue ricochets like the puck in a hockey game. We moved out of one on the second day, rehearsing *A Man for All Seasons* last year in London.

By any measure, the rehearsal hall here at the PAT is world class. For one thing, it's very large, with high ceilings and no mirrors or windows . . . you get good sound. They also gave me a very good rehearsal set, with real furniture and platforms; this last week, the actual pieces as they came out of the shop. This is absolutely verboten with the technical unions back home, unless you lay on a standby crew of stagehands. I've rehearsed love scenes on Broadway using three folding chairs. The unions have been forced to give way on this issue recently, but it was a pleasure to come to China and find a rehearsal set with stairs and desks and doors that worked. Ask any actor.

OCTOBER 13th Thursday Rehearsal Day #22

First Day on Stage
1:30 Tech Act I
4:30 Break
6:00 Tech Act II
10:00 PM finish

Today, I moved the company sixty yards down the hall onto the stage. (There are very few Western theatres with adequate—or any—rehearsal facilities in the same building.) The People's Art Theatre is a large compound, with double iron gates leading to the forecourt of the theatre. It's very impressive: a firm cultural edifice, Western style, circa late 19th/early 20th century. It was built in 1950, just after the triumph of the revolution. They must've had a lot more money then. Just yesterday, the government announced they were cutting off, temporarily, all funding for construction in the arts, including a few projects already under way. Well, we've already got this theatre. It could use a coat of paint and a general cleanup, but it's better as a stage machine than many theatres I know in the West. There's no marquee (I've not seen one in China), but they have our signs up, very handsome in swashing Chinese characters, and a flight of broad, shallow steps up into a lobby that looks like an opera house: sweeping stairways, chandeliers, marble pillars. I've played in theatres that would fit inside it.

An extremely gifted mimic, particularly in female roles, Yang Lixin played the pompous psychiatrist, Bird. Here Greenwald (Ren Baoxian) traps him into revealing his inconsistencies.

The theatre itself is large, some fourteen hundred seats, including a balcony. There're a number of seats on the sides with terrible sight lines, especially for our set. I walked the whole house, above and below, and marked the seats they mustn't sell. The orchestra pit and the deep forestage are also problems . . . separating the audience from the play. Nothing I can do about that. The acoustics, though, are marvelous. Acoustics are more mystery than science . . . they got very lucky here.

I could use a little science onstage. There's plenty of room for our set and it looks fine (after I took out a window unit that ruined the party set at the end). I'd give my thumb (well, maybe a little toe) for a proper intercom connection with the backstage workstations. (It'd be swell if I could speak Chinese, too.) Even with Mme. Xie, it's much harder to translate messages yelled at stagehands forty feet up in the flies than to discuss the intricacies of a scene with an actor standing beside you.

I left the actors to play through more or less on their own tonight, while I concentrated on the technical problems. Still, we teched through the entire play in a long afternoon session and a shorter evening one. That's not bad, in any terms. I've done plays that took two full days to tech. I'm giving the cast the morning off tomorrow.

OCTOBER 14th Friday Rehearsal Day #23

2nd Tech
9:00 Watch 2nd Bush-Dukakis debate in suite, live on CNN
6:30 To theatre
7:00 Tech
10:20 Wrap

Since I'd given the actors a late call, we had time to sit in the suite and watch the last Bush-Dukakis debate live on CNN. (Impossible ten years ago, now routine, even here.) It wasn't remarkable. (They seldom are . . . even candidates with overwhelming TV chemistry, like RR, tend to play defensive ball-control in these high-risk situations.) Bush did that this morning (last evening, in L.A.), as of course he should, protecting a lead.

Our breakfast constituency of two thought he did that. He was easier, seemed more assured, with a certain weight, yet readier for a light comeback. Dukakis was still tight (as he has reason to be). He can't do anything about his eyebrows, but someone should talk to him about his rapid pace, the down-stresses at the end of each sentence, constantly accented by double hand-chops. Certainly, both men did better, but Bush more so, I think. That's a professional judgment of performance . . . what I do for a living. Never doubt that political leadership, particularly at that level, requires performance.

I made my political choice some time ago, as I suppose most people did. For me, aside from the last eight years and the next eight (plus the Soviets), it turned on Dukakis's insistence that his election is about competence, not ideology. What the hell are we trying to do here . . . run the Municipal Waterworks?

The weather changed today. We're working indoors, so you have to keep an eye out, but if we'd been filming on location, you couldn't have missed it. Going out of the hotel, down to the corner where Mr. Li picks me up to avoid the tourists in the lobby, there was a stiff, twenty-knot wind with an edge in it, pulling the leaves off the trees. "The northwest wind!" he said, "from Mongolia! . . ." gesturing elaborately, the way you explain things to children. "Soon it will be winter!" he said, pantomiming the cold. I explained I'd been raised near Canada ("Eeeaugh! The North Pole!"), and anyway we'd be gone in a few weeks. But as we drove to the theatre, many of the bicyclists had red cheesecloth wrapped round their heads. "To keep out the dust!" Mr. Li said. I'm not sure it would do that.

The run-through went pretty well. "You could open tomorrow!" Yeah . . . so they say. Actually, we're in very good shape, which is why I'm working them so little. Jimmy Doolittle's in town now; I appreciate a fresh, professional eye on things. I need more from Queeg, a little less from Greenwald; I have to straighten out the party scene and a lot of technical sloppiness, but we'll be fine. I sent them home early.

James Doolittle, manager of the Doolittle Theatre in Holly-
wood, is a lover of all things Chinese. Chuck and Jimmy are
seated in the Great Wall Hotel, discussing plans for opening
night. (Jimmy had been crucial in arranging for the presenta-
tion of **The Caine Mutiny Court-martial** *in Beijing.)*

OCTOBER 15th Saturday Rehearsal Day #24

LAST TECH
9:30 Stills for People *layout: here, and at Forbidden City*
11:00 Forbidden City: opening Acousti-guide tour
1:30 Lunch w/Lydia
5:30 Notes to actors
6:00 Check all makeup, uniforms, and props
7:30 Full technical rehearsal
10:00 Final curtain. Technical notes w/crew & staff

I let the cast rest this morning; Lydia and I went over to watch Bette Lord and Ying Ruocheng inaugurate the Acousti-guide Tour of the Forbidden City (for which he'd done the Mandarin narration). That's the outfit I narrated the *Rameses the Great* audiocassette for last year. They do a good job. Their cassettes take you through an exhibition better than most tour guides can. (And why not, with the likes of Peter Ustinov and old what's'name doing the voice over?) While we were there, I did a few more stills for Lydia, as well as for *People* magazine. Their layout seems to grow by the day. (I'll believe it when I see it in print.) **[It turned out to be quite a piece . . . several admiring pages and good photo coverage.]**

Before I went to the theatre, I had a little time with Herman Wouk and his wife, Sarah, who had just got in for the opening. I'm very pleased he wanted to come. Of course, they came to the tech tonight, as did Lydia (well cameraed) and the other people who've made this happen. This was in theory a technical run-through, but there must've been 150 people in the house, mostly drama students, with some oth-

As the authoritative squadron commander Captain Southard, Mi Tiezeng registered strongly.

Yang Lixin, playing the smug psychiatrist, Bird. Although psychiatry is not popular in China, Lixin's audiences understood him completely and laughed with the same enthusiasm as our audiences did in Los Angeles and London.

ers as well, including, I was startled to find, the critics. I began to bristle at this, given the adversarial function of critics in the West, when Bette Lord explained that critics here always saw at least three performances before they wrote their reviews. They also hope to meet with me, as well as Wouk, before they publish. I'm staggered. Here, I suppose, is Oriental intellectualism at its considering, contemplative best.

Frank Rich and Dan Sullivan would hoot at this, of course. They feel no need to consult with the people who made the work before issuing their papal bulls . . . (isn't that a good noun here?). Besides, they have deadlines! It'd be useful, though . . . a lot better than the "Critic, the Killer Rabbit" system we have at home.

Actually, the final tech could've been the final dress rehearsal. The performances were right on the edge. Another two hours of work and they'll be ready. Some of the sound cues were sloppy. (The foghorn/sea gull punctuation is delicate and they don't have it yet, but we're close.) The cake frosting was a disaster; it'd congealed before Greenwald tried to wipe it across Keefer's face, but that's easy to fix.

Herman Wouk seemed genuinely delighted. He came up on stage and talked to the cast afterward, lifting their hearts high. (Mine, too.) In the end, this is the opinion that counts the most . . . what the people who did the work think of it.

After I'd dismissed the actors and given them tomorrow off, we had what could've been a really serious confrontation. Bette Bao Lord came up to me in the little huddle of technicians sorting through the glitches. "Chuck," she said. "There's a problem." She often says that to me and then proceeds to solve it herself, with the energy and dedication of a tigress. This seemed different. "You said it was OK to have photographers in the front row for the preview tomorrow?"

"That's right. I'm not enchanted with the idea, but you

said we've had an awful lot of requests for coverage."

"But there are four photographers who want to shoot on opening night, too."

"Too bad," I said. "They can't." Well, we then had about fifteen minutes on this, increasingly impassioned on the Chinese side (not Bette Lord; she did her extraordinary best to mediate). I saw this was one I had to win, for the play. You don't do that by getting mad, or yelling. Tough counts a lot.

"Please tell me one shot you can get on opening night that you can't get the night before, with the other twenty-seven photographers?" I asked. Well . . . the shots of the speeches afterward and the presentation of the flowers.

"Fine, you can shoot the flowers. But if one of you takes out a camera during the performance on opening night, I will personally throw you out of the theatre. I am able to do that. I *will* do that."

It was clear by then that the only reason these four guys wanted to shoot opening night was to demonstrate that they could shoot when nobody else could. For some curious reason, they are the official government photographers. I sensed a move to postpone it all and somehow slip it through tomorrow, when the big broken-nosed round-eye had forgotten about it. The theatre manager, a perfectly fine man, cleared his throat and said equably, "Well, we will talk to the board."

"Don't do that," I said. "This discussion is over. On opening night, the play belongs to the actors and the audience. There will be no photographers during the performance." All this was painfully thrown back and forth over the language barrier, which never seemed too high. As I turned to go out to the car, I said to Bette Lord, who can read these things from both sides, "Be sure they understand this, Bette. Please. I've been infinitely flexible on a lot of problems . . . painting the stage floor, intercoms, better tapes . . . things they can't afford. That's fine. *This* is nothing but vanity. I won't damage the play and distract the actors for that. I just drew a line in the dust. No further. Believe me."

It wasn't really a large problem, of course. If this was our only major difference . . . and it was . . . it means the whole cross-cultural, international undertaking has worked. It has. After I discussed the whole thing with Lydia, she said, as I turned out the light, "Maybe Herman Wouk can help you on this."

"I don't need any help, honey," I said. "We're OK now."

OCTOBER 16th Sunday Day Off

1:30 w/Lydia to the Temple of Heaven

We had the stage available for rehearsal on the set today, but I canceled the call. The company's so close to ready, I want to leave them with things still to do when we finish the preview tomorrow. I didn't even give them my notes after rehearsal last night. "I see you stand like greyhounds in the slips/Straining upon the start." Yeah, they do. Henry V's troops at Agincourt.

Lydia and I went to the Temple of Heaven this afternoon. (She'd seen it with Maggie before.) It's an awesome place, where through the centuries emperors came during the change of seasons to perform sacrificial rituals in hope of a good harvest. I think it's the most beautiful single building I've seen so far in China. On top of a hill, it rises in concentric halos of blue tile. Today was Sunday, so it was jammed not only with the daily flood of tourists, but with the Chinese whose heritage it is.

Prominent among the many rituals of the Chinese imperial period was the winter solstice sacrifice, performed annually in the central room of this temple, where the emperor took the sins of his people on himself, cleansing them of this burden for the next year in the hope of a better harvest.

A thousand years ago, this was more than a symbolic acceptance of guilt ritually assumed by the ruler; there seem to have been times when he was literally sacrificed. A thousand years before that, Christ died on the cross to cleanse the sins of man. Two thousand years before *that*, the brutal matriarchal societies of Bronze Age Greece slaughtered their Year King annually and plowed his blood and flesh into the seeded fields. These things occur to you in a place as old as this. **[The blood shed in Tiananmen Square a few months later and indeed throughout Chinese history, from the Communists back through the Manchus, is perhaps more comprehensible in these terms.]**

In spite of all this, the pervasive human presence here on this Sunday were the children, overwhelming the ghosts and shadows. There must've been a thousand Chinese families in the compounds, each with one child chasing another, shrieking with laughter, sliding down the marble balustrades, smooth with centuries. They stood still only to have their pictures taken against the looming imperial steps, their parents beaming with pride as they arranged them. I noticed how unusually handsome the children were, better dressed, often, than their parents. I realized at last that all these five-year-olds, boys and girls alike, were wearing full makeup, rouge, lipstick, and eye shadow. Amazing! **[Later, I found that, in a country where the government sharply limits the number of children permitted, mandating abortion for extra pregnancies, the single child allowed life in each family is treasured beyond measure. Perhaps the makeup is a gesture of freedom, of the value of the individual child, against the faceless commonality of the Cultural Revolution.]**

Back at the hotel, we had a pleasant dinner with the Wouks and Jimmy Doolittle, trading easy, bantering stories about plays we'd done, halfway around the world from where we'd done them. (Lydia and I had done Herman's first play, *The Traitor*, some thirty years ago.) There was little talk about *Caine*. I think we all feel it's coming just about right, just about now. Which is when it should.

OCTOBER 17th Monday Dress Rehearsal Day #25

10:00 Rehearsal call
12:15 Break
7:00 Dress rehearsal
11:00 PM Drink w/Wouks, J. Doolittle . . . hotel

I'm very proud of them all . . . actors, staff, crew. We worked a couple of hours this morning, cleaning up bits and pieces, then had a show-smooth dress rehearsal with an audience. Tonight, we could've opened. I gave no notes afterward, just a call for tomorrow at 5:00 PM. (At home, I'd call the company for 11:00 AM, then give them the afternoon off; but here most of them commute to the theatre an hour or more by bicycle, and they don't want two round-trips.) Anyway, I don't have as much to say as they think I do; I just have to keep them up for it. It's like the Super Bowl . . . they've got to be sharp and hungry. All of them.

We did this in 25 working days, including tonight. Two and a half of those days were spent reworking the Chinese text to make it shorter, more colloquial. They were prepared; they were able·and eager to work. You can't ask for more.

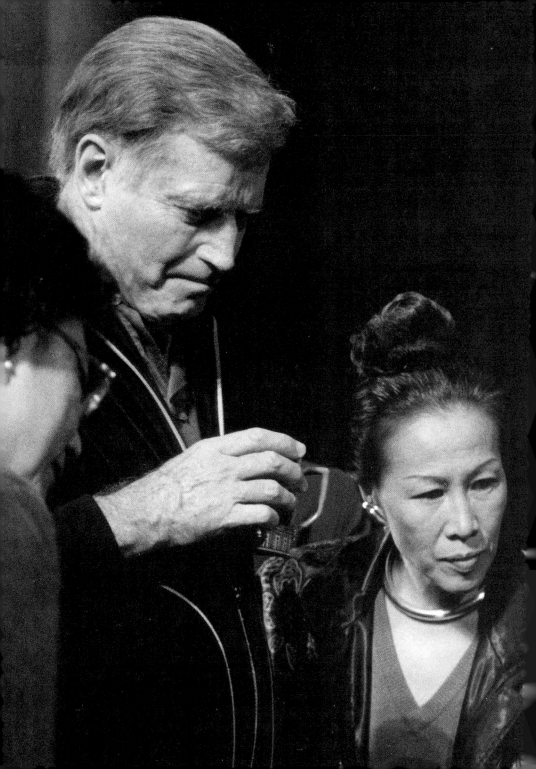

OCTOBER 18th Tuesday Opening Night Beijing

You can't really understand about opening nights unless you've opened some. The media describe it very well from the other side: the Beautiful People and the limos and lights, but they don't get into what it's like for the people who are actually opening.

I think there's a parallel with athletes: a lot of it is absolute belief. I once spent the morning with Rod Laver before one of his Grand Slam finals. Rocket's one of the great athletes of all time; the Laurence Olivier of tennis. He was relaxed and rested, in the best of Aussie high spirits. He obviously couldn't wait to play the match. The thought that he might lose it never crossed his mind. He didn't. Of course. Early in the tournament, I'd asked him whom he'd likely meet in the later rounds. "I dunno, Blue," he said. "Players . . ." That's how Olivier felt, opening in *Othello*.

Acting is not supposed to be a competitive undertaking. It is, though . . . unavoidably. First, it's for scholarships and prizes in sonnet-reading. Later on, you can't help but keep track of the other guys. Wasn't it Gore Vidal who said, "When anyone else succeeds, you die a little"? That's Vidal, of course, but sometimes you do catch yourself thinking, "Christ, I should've done that part after all . . . look at the grosses. I would've been better in it, too." Tennis players have it a little easier . . . they only have to win.

In truth, though, actors compete only with themselves, and with the part. If you're doing one of Shakespeare's mon-

Bette Bao Lord and Chuck ruminating during first dress rehearsal.

ster man-killers, you're also competing with four centuries of work on it, and what everyone's thought about it all that time. If you're dealing with a modern piece like *Caine,* the well-remembered film version spends only some twelve minutes with the court-martial that takes up our entire play. Not many people even remember that Hank Fonda was the original Greenwald, the play's protagonist on stage, but a small role in the film. Happily, here in China no one's seen either the play or the film, so we have a clean slate.

I felt a little raggedy during the day, for no good reason. I played a little tennis, but I still felt edgy, which isn't like me. I've always identified with Albert the alligator, in Walt Kelly's treasured comic strip *Pogo.* When Pogo asks Albert if he's ever thought much about "the inner me," he says, "Naw. I got 'nough trouble with th' me whut's out'cheer whar I kin git muh hands on 'im. As fer the inner me . . . he goes his way, I go mine."

Then I realized what was eating me. I wasn't going to get to act! This is the first play I've directed in years where I didn't also play a part. I love directing, but acting is what I *do!* It's like wining and dining and dancing with the lady, then taking her back to her door after the ball . . . where she turns her cheek for a kiss and goes to bed alone. The analogy is not idle; when it comes off, there's something sexual about performance. Especially on stage; to have one of the monster Shakespearean soliloquies really happen is . . . yes, orgasmic. A successful scene with someone else is even better (again, like sex).

On the other hand, I can't act in Mandarin. Happily, I have some fine actors who can. At five o'clock, I went round to the dressing rooms to deliver my opening night gifts and bring them up to the edge. When you want to encourage an actor, go to his dressing room . . . that's his country; as director, you're a guest there. It helps. They all looked good; they sounded ready. I envied them the pleasures of performance.

Gu Wei (center) as Blakely, the judge, and other members of the court.

Yang Lixin (Bird) protests to Wu Guiling (Challee).

Captain Queeg's final defeat as Ren Baoxian (Greenwald)
hands him the very report Queeg himself had submitted,
praising Maryk for his character and seamanship.

It was really fine . . . the best they've given. We peaked at the right time . . . like Rod Laver or Joe Montana. We seem to be a very hot ticket, which doesn't mean a lot when they go for fifty cents each. (Fifty dollars now, on Broadway, which kind of crowds out the kids and the working stiffs back home.)

I was prepared for the usual opening night gefuffle . . . people coming late, VIPs, and flash shots. I had no idea so much of the audience would be ordinary people in shirt-sleeves and tennis shoes. Also, I'd never really thought through the question of whether Herman Wouk's examination of how democracy works, even within the confines of the military, could communicate with a people unacquainted with democracy. For the several millennia of their recorded history, the Chinese have been ruled by a variety of authoritarian governments, usually savagely oppressive. The current Communist regime seems to provide the most fertile ground for the ideas in Wouk's play.

[My autumn optimism was dashed a few months later in Tiananmen Square, but, like so many errors in judgment, it seemed like a good idea at the time.]

This audience gave us what playmakers prize most: attention. I'd been warned that Chinese audiences tended to be noisy, talking among themselves (like Western movie audiences). This one was raptly attentive, perhaps concentrating on following unfamiliar situations and characters. The comedy . . . and there is some in *Caine,* very adroitly placed . . . worked, too, canceling a major worry. (Believe me, comedy in translation is slippery as soap.)

After the curtain calls (shouts, flowers, your classic

Zhu Xu in the moment of Queeg's insane fury against his crew.

standing O), we had the speeches and then the press backstage, in the kind of feeding frenzy I've seen happen a couple of times. It had nothing to do with how good the production was or how much the audience liked it . . . the assembled media (mostly Western) simply decided to record a triumph and then created it more or less on their own. The press reception was a madhouse, with one photographer breaking through the table he was standing on.

I was glad to retreat in a flurry of flashbulbs to the cast reception, where I got to pass out the company jackets with the *Caine* logo. (My actors had never heard of what is now expected custom in the West. They really need good jackets, too, with winter coming on. I picked warm ones on purpose.) They were happy, I was proud. The Old Gentleman in Stratford had it right, as usual: "A hit, a very palpable hit."

Celebrating his great triumph, the publication of his novel, the true villain, Keefer (Xiu Zongdi), raises his glass of champagne in praise of himself.

Charlton Heston: Adapted from Herman Wouk's novel *The Caine Mutiny*, the play deals with the court-martial of Lieutenant Maryk, executive officer of the *Caine*, for taking command of the ship during a typhoon at the height of World War II, relieving a captain he believed to be psychopathic. Maryk is defended by a grounded naval aviator, Lieutenant Greenwald, who describes himself as "a damn good lawyer and a pretty poor flyer." In the course of what seems an open-and-shut case against Maryk, a parade of witnesses, some foolish, some expert and decent men, reveals Captain Queeg as flawed and desperate. Greenwald, in a tactic from which he ethically recoils, succeeds in making Queeg, not Maryk, the accused. It's an extraordinary play, exploring Queeg's devastating disintegration at the same time it explores the dilemma of democracy at war.

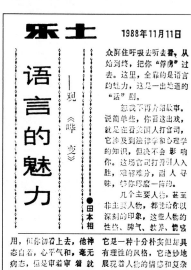

Beijing Youth Daily, November 11, 1988
"SEDUCTION BY WORDS"
Review by Tian Benxiang

To the young people of the capital, I recommend a top-notch play —Oscar winning actor Charlton Heston's production of *The Caine Mutiny*.

If offers no dazzling scenery, no disco numbers, no break dancing, no female roles. It is simply a story of naval officers and navy men. Moreover, nearly the whole play takes place in a military courtroom, with little action to speak of. That's about it. Yet a hush reigns in the theater. The audience is held captive from start to finish. . . .

话剧《哗变》涉及的主题对于今日的中国人应不算陌生——当一代激进好斗的年轻人在老人与规矩压抑时，理性的选择应该是什么？

《哗变》在玩弄一个巧妙而诡谲的法庭论辩之后，给了我们一个十分保守的答复，创作者认为下级对上级普遍的抵触情绪是缺乏责任感的，当一个国家需要保卫时，即使是心理不太健全的平庸之辈（如魁格舰长之流）也应该肯定的。知识分子（尤其是青年）那种毫无本能的厌战或反战举动是非理性而无聊的。

《哗变》在谴责哗变时设置了一个不容颠覆的前提——战争状态。尽管小说家基弗可以认为战争是荒唐无聊的，是迄今为止人类理性所能操纵的最无理性的事件，但战争法则却自有其无情的规律。它要求双方以最高的智力和最广的人力去赢得战争，它需要刻板的规章制度和严明的纪律约束，更需要千百万魁格舰长式的"庸才"投身其中并执行由"天才"创造的"海军制度"。此刻，嘲笑它的愚蠢本身便是某种愚蠢，青年人激进地追求卓越的造反行径只会带来破坏性的结局，文人墨客的幻灭感和玩世感在此毫无用处。

《哗变》在得出上述结论的时候毫不犹豫，格林渥律师在终场戏中的痛斥，令小说家基弗汗颜。然而让人困惑不解的地方在于，当最终的结论出现以前，观众的判断已经完全倒向了反秩序反理性的青年人一方，格林渥律师的辩才彻底扭曲了现实的本来面目，人类"理性的误区"使得法庭这种理性的殿堂反成了反理性的市场。也许有人会从中看出法律本身的荒谬，但对于坚信良知和道德的人们而言，它实际上表达了一种更为深刻的怀疑，人类的公平和正义有可能通过理性的道路实现吗？

崇尚科学理性和习惯于破旧立新的中国观众面对《哗变》恐怕会感到为难，在缺乏实证精神的环境里难道不需要高扬理性的旗帜吗？面对僵硬的教条和古老的传统难道不需要革新精神吗？这真是一个意味深长的命题，当着一个民族正为赶上西方国家并打赢经济上的战争而拼命奋战时，《哗变》的出现实在是件令人尴尬的事情。

选择的误区

杨平

Beijing Evening News, October 25, 1988
"THE FALLACY OF CHOICE"
by Yang Ping

The theme dealt with in *The Caine Mutiny Court-martial* is not strange to today's Chinese: What should be the rational choice of a group of very young men weighed down by an older generation and its strictures?

The answer given by the play—after an intricate, often cunning, court debate—is most conservative. . . . In condemning the act of mutiny, *Caine* sets up the precondition for conflict—a state of war. . . . To win, both sides must marshal their greatest forces of intelligence and manpower with the utmost discipline. . . . Mocking the folly of war is a kind of folly in itself. Youth's relentless pursuit of rebellion can only lead to disastrous results; intellectual snobbery, a sense of disillusionment, and skepticism are pointless.

. . . But before this conclusion is brought out, the audience's sympathy is inclined toward the rebellious youths through Greenwald's manipulation of the facts. The fallacy of "human reason" turns the court—the palace of reason—into a forum of antireason. . . . Moreover, further doubts are raised—can human justice and righteousness be realized through rational means?

A Chinese audience, versed in scientific reason and accustomed to "destroying the old to make way for the new," is bound to find itself in a dilemma while watching *Caine*. When the search for truth lapses, shouldn't the flag of reason be raised? In the face of rigid dogma and outdated traditions, isn't revolutionary spirit called for? For a nation struggling desperately for victory in an economic war to catch up with the western world, the arrival of *The Caine Mutiny Court-martial* is extremely awkward.

CHINA JOURNAL, BOOK 4
10/19/88–10/27/88

OCTOBER 19th Wednesday USIA Tour Day #1

9:00 China Film Ass'n (CFA): symposium on film
1:00 Beijing Film Studios: tour lot, run films
6:00 Zamora dinner—French restaurant in hotel

My job with *Caine* done, I began earning the modest share
of my expenses in China that the USIA is picking up to have
me take a look at the Chinese film industry and "interface"
(what a dumb word) with film people here. I still have Mr.
Li and his ice-blue Shanghai to get around in and, most
crucially, Mme. Xie to translate the torrents of talk, but this
is Barbara Zigli's show now, for the State Department.

We started off at the China Film Association's headquar-
ters, where I was met by an impressive delegation of offi-
cials. Introductions were performed and we filed into a
square room furnished only with low tables and square, upholstered chairs lining all the walls, with Victorian lace anti-
macassars (like the chairs you see our presidents sitting in
when they go to China on state visits). Tea was served,
meticulously, in tiny, fragile porcelain. Everyone sipped
once and placed the cup on the table.

A silence ensued. (The Chinese are good at silences.)
Presently, I was welcomed formally and responded, punc-
tuated by translation. There was a discussion about the importance of film in world culture, its value as a mind-shaping
tool . . . all pretty high-flown. I was thanked for my contribution to Chinese theatre. (These were film people; they
weren't at the opening.) Still, I was impressed. This is what
summit meetings must be like.

It's amazing how many chiefs they have in Communist
countries. Look at all those guys in the hats on the Kremlin

wall on May Day . . . a hundred, easy. Maybe it's the insistence on full employment; all the major intersections in Beijing have four policemen directing traffic from a concrete island in the center.

Certainly everyone seems to have a job, though I gather he doesn't have any say about what it is. The estimable Mr. Li tells me he was assigned to motor mechanics school at fourteen. ("Oh, shoot. I was counting on chemist. Could I check again next week, maybe?" "Gee, sorry. We had some chemistry slots the other day. Only drivers right now.")

We then proceeded to Beijing Film Studios, to be greeted by another delegation, the ritual similar to this morning except that after the tea, we had small, dubious sandwiches and rice wine, followed by a tour of the studio, which is like all other studios I've ever seen—slightly out of date (considerably so, here), dusty and cluttered, repeated warnings not to trip on the cables I've been avoiding before the people who warn me were born.

Some of the sets from *The Last Emperor* are still standing . . . absolutely world class. On the back lot, some really fine exterior sets are now useless because the sky behind them is now studded with high-rise buildings. That happened a long time ago in Hollywood. It's curious how similar film studios are around the world. Over a drink at the hotel tonight with the Wouks and Jimmy Doolittle, someone asked Lydia about the *Ben-Hur* shoot. "How marvelous to have ten months in Rome!" "It was for me," Lydia said, "but Chuck didn't have ten months in Rome. He had ten months at Cinecitta Studios."

Euphoric with our success here, we explored the idea of taking *Caine* to Moscow, with a Russian company. That would be a challenge, surely (but not right now, Lord!).

[Not long after we got back from China, I found myself doing a film in Europe and North Africa. I had no time to

148

think about taking the *Caine* to Moscow till I got home again in March. I talked to Jimmy Doolittle then, and he explored his considerable contacts in the Soviet Union. High excitement . . . yes, they were very interested.

We were a meeting away from agreement. As in China, of course, I would work free, but that seems to be the basic Communist presumption of capitalists. I was all for it. The weather was likely to be lousy and the food and creature comforts wouldn't compare to China, but the theatrical talent pool in Moscow is extraordinary. Also, the Russian acting style, while a little presentational by our standards, is closer to what we do here than the Chinese perception. The chance to work with actors trained in the distinguished tradition of the Moscow Art Theatre would be a valuable learning experience for me. (When I was studying acting at Northwestern, Konstantin Stanislavski's *An Actor Prepares* was our Bible.)

Besides, having directed and acted *Caine* in London, L.A., and Washington, to mount indigenous companies in both Beijing and Moscow would be something of a hat trick (whatever that means, but I know it's good). I looked forward to it.

First, I had yet another acting job, in my son's film of *Treasure Island.* During the English shoot, I tried to connect with the Soviet Minister of Culture, but I was off to location in Jamaica before he got to London. One of the problems of art in the socialist countries is that everything has to be cleared at a very high bureaucratic level. It's like having to check with the State Department before you film *Honey, I Shrunk the Kids.* I also missed the Wimbledon final again. (Not the Soviets' fault.)

Treasure Island finished (for me, at least; Fraser was directing this one), I got back to California just as the Soviet culture honcho got here. Well, not here, but in San Francisco, with a ballet company. Would I fly up to close the deal, asked Jimmy Doolittle? You bet. Fifty minutes on a plane, two hours to wrap it up, home again in half a day. Piece of cake.

So Jimmy and I flew up to San Francisco, found the Soviets' hotel easily . . . but no minister. Russian/English speakers were thin on the ground, too; the one we found was not very forthcoming. Yes, certainly the minister was here, though not at this moment in the hotel, nor was it clear when he might return. Yes, the minister was aware of our meeting, certainly he would be back . . . very shortly.

We waited an hour. Then I took a cab to the airport and flew back to L.A., feeling ill-used. Jimmy waited another hour, met the minister in the lobby, who was full of apology and reassurance. Since then, there's been no contact.

This was only weeks after Tiananmen Square, which says a great deal, I think. The Chinese certainly don't blame our little undertaking for that massive convulsion, but the Soviets are chess players. Teetering on the edge of the same sort of bloody blunder, they really don't need a play exploring the ideas *Caine* does. In their place, I guess I wouldn't let me in, either. Besides, I *know* I couldn't get any peanut butter in Moscow.]

OCTOBER 20th Thursday USIA Tour Day #2

I spent the morning at the Beijing Film Academy, where China is training her filmmakers. The pressure for places there is even greater than at home: They have some ten thousand applicants for a student body of six hundred students. (There are three hundred professors . . . that's a helluva good student/teacher ratio.)

I was at a little of a loss as to how to reach the acting class I was asked to share. Never mind the language barrier; almost no one in China has ever seen or heard of me; why should they pay attention to a big round-eye? I talked to them a little, then decided the best thing would be an improvisation, as we used to do in acting classes. Improvisation is a lot like masturbation: It's fun, but it doesn't really accomplish much. Still, it introduces you to the process.

To make it work, you have to give the actors conflicting goals in the scene. I told the boy I picked that he was a studio head who had to tell a major film star she couldn't have the role she expected in his next film. I told the girl, separately, of course, that as an aging star she had to have the part, and knew she could force it because they'd been lovers.

Oddly, it didn't work. Neither the boy nor the girl would drive the scene to real confrontation. I'm no sinologist; I have no idea whether this has anything to do with China or the Chinese. Maybe they were just scared.

After lunch at the hotel with my girl, I went to the theatre for a seminar with the critics. This was a new experience . . . one on twenty with the enemy, face to face. (You have to bear in mind that actors regard critics as antagonists, bent on depriving them of employment overnight, lacking either the capacity or the time to reach rational judgment. I did a play with Laurence Olivier once where the notices killed us before the opening night party was over. Commiserating with him over a brandy, I said, "Well, I suppose you learn to ignore the bad notices." He gripped my elbow fiercely and said, "Laddie . . . it's much harder, and much more important, to learn to ignore the good ones.")

That's what we have to concentrate on now, anyway . . . ignoring the good ones. The critics had all seen the play at least twice, and they all thought we were the cat's pajamas. Hell, I'll sign that. Like everyone else, I've had good notices and I've had bad. Never mind whether they know what they're talking about, good is better.

It was unique, in my experience, to sit around a table for two hours talking about a play and what you've done with it, to the people who've written about it. I don't suppose we'll ever see the like of that at home. I think American critics prefer their Olympian message-from-the-mountain method.

OCTOBER 21st Friday USIA Tour Day #3

9:00 China Film Ass'n (CFA): seminar with filmmakers
2:00 Lunch w/Lydia pack bags for shipment to U.S.
4:30 Bags out

I spent the day meeting with the honchos of the China Film Association (who are picking up part of the tab for this USIA mini-tour we're launched on) plus some filmmakers. Over thirty-some years of setting up and attending such affairs, I've become very skeptical about the usefulness of any meeting with more than six people. (Yeah, the United Nations and the U.S. Congress, too.) As the number involved rises, so does the level of bullshit. At the UN, I'd say it gets to about ninety-two percent. This morning in the CFA conference room (you have to add about five percent just for being in a formal conference room), with twenty people in attendance, I'd say bullshit to substance split maybe 60/40, which is pretty good, actually.

The sixty percent was spent discussing film as art . . . the 20th century's art form, the American art form, et cetera, et cetera. All true, but we've all heard and said that before. I even got in Lenin's prescient definition of film as the most powerful weapon ever forged to shape the mind of man. (That is by God true . . . it also goes down well with a Communist audience.)

We did get into substance, then . . . how films are made and sold, the problems of a subsidized film industry. I'm coming to believe subsidizing anything dooms it to failure, but at the same time, I've spent a lot of my life lobbying for and then doling out taxpayers' money to subsidize the arts at home, including film.

With subsidy, you can give opportunity; you have to be careful about giving security. Especially in film and theatre, total security cuts you off from your audience, because you don't need to please them anymore. It's a thorny problem: to stimulate, but not smother.

For the Chinese, total subsidy is mandatory, not only as socialist dogma, but because the price of a movie ticket is pegged at about four cents. (At home, movie tickets now cost seven dollars . . . that's almost seventeen thousand percent higher.) The government thus has to pick up the whole tab for the Chinese film industry, as is the case in the Soviet Union. It isn't impossible to make good films this way, but it's tougher. Bureaucrats and apparatchiks tend to make the choices. Given all this, and a somewhat worn technology, the Chinese have still made some good films.

I got back to the hotel early enough to give Lydia a hand with the packing (some bags straight to L.A., a few with us on the tour). Then, we had a farewell dinner with the Lords, who brought us over here; the Zamoras, who put us up; and the Corcorans, who smoothed the way. Pat Corcoran's next posting will be in Florence . . . he's already begun his Italian lessons. Marvelous people, all of them. We couldn't have done this without them.

OCTOBER 22nd Saturday USIA Tour Day #4

Travel: BEIJING TO XI'AN

This morning, while I was packing, the desk called up to say that the *Caine* company was in the lobby. So they were, almost every man of them, most of them wearing their *Caine Mutiny* jackets, having bicycled and bused across Beijing to say goodbye to me. I was deeply, deeply touched. I've never had a company that worked harder (or *had* to work harder, for that matter, since they had to figure out what the hell I was talking about, for openers). To do this play in Chinese, for a Chinese audience, required an enormous reach. They supplied most of that. They made Herman's play work.

Flying us across the Pacific to Beijing, the Chinese government airline performed admirably, competing as they must with other international carriers outside China. On interior flights, they have no competition. The difference is startling. We had two reservations today; neither served us well. Our noon flight was inexplicably canceled; the 6:45 PM flight was three hours late, losing another twenty minutes en route. It was a Russian Ilyushin, which was a little daunting. Flying to Xi'an, my seat was as cramped as any I ever flew in, except in the back of an A5 with the Blue Angels . . . and that was at least fun. Between my knees and the back of the man in the seat ahead was only two inches of padding. I don't know which of us was in more pain.

We finally checked into the elegant Golden Flower Hotel in Xi'an three hours late, scrubbing a couple of interviews for the USIA. A cool pillow under your head feels good at the end of a day like this.

OCTOBER 23rd Sunday Day #5 (Free)

Tour XI'AN

This Sunday was downtime for us . . . no work. We used it to explore the vast army of life-sized terra-cotta warriors buried here by the Emperor Qin Shi Huangdi two centuries before Christ. Thousands were discovered here in 1974, sleeping through two millennia under the clay, armed and mounted for combat.

No one has explained the purpose of this vast undertaking. Had the emperor himself died, they would surely have simply interred his live soldiers as bodyguards in the afterworld. Possibly he had these clay soldiers created to honor his mother's death, to lie buried on perpetual alert, leaving him live troops to serve more usefully above ground.

The dig is a vast, roofed acreage of excavation, with hushed throngs of visitors moving on catwalks ten feet

A line of terra-cotta soldiers near Xi'an, buried for three thousand years. Photographs are strictly forbidden here, but my quiet Canon's autofocus can't read signs. I bought dozens of color slides to ease my conscience. (I thought of the gracious British Museum in London, where anything may be photographed, as long as no tripod or flash is used. It's a different philosophy.) The soldiers, life-size and impressive beyond belief, are still not entirely excavated, with the possibility of thousands more to be found. Each is unique, with differing hair and features. Were they sculpted from life?

above the ancient earth where the clay soldiers are only beginning to be uncovered.

What you mark most, I think, are the individual faces, all surely portraits of specific men . . . archer, officer, cavalryman, each distinct in the multitude. The curious realism of the figures is enhanced by the thin winter light washing over the cratered landscape of the dig. It looks like a battlefield. There are squads lying broken like men after a firefight, strewn in random sprawls of death, and phalanxes of figures still chest-deep in dirt, as if they were fording a river. But these countless clay columns stand for men, ready to be buried for the emperor. Did he ever think of them? Why did he make pottery clones to spare them? The men he saved crumbled to dust two thousand years ago, but their clay doubles have waited here all this time for us to come and look at them.

Lydia came well cameraed, of course, but we were all daunted by the fiercest signs forbidding photography I've ever seen . . . in several languages, featuring phrases like "absolutely prohibited" and "violators will be punished." Well, tough luck, I thought. She'll buy some postcards. Not my girl. She has her Nikon strapped to her hip, burning film past the lens on auto focus like a KGB agent at a nuclear sub base.

"DAR-ling," I began.

"SHHHHSH!" she hissed. Mme. Xie seized her shoulder. (We were all huddled around her now like a human tent.)

"Mrs. Heston . . . this is really dangerous. They will take your camera! At least!"

"SHHHHSH!" Lydia replied, looking around serenely while she flicked the shutter through her open jacket. Incredibly, none of the guards noticed. (She was an actress, after all.) She ran the whole roll through and, to my relief, decided against trying to reload under her jacket. (They'd have thought she was having a baby.)

In Xi'an we visited the military museum of the Long March of 1949, which marked the victory of Chinese Communism. One hundred twenty thousand men set off from Canton; only 30,000 survived the march to the north. Thinking to amuse his friend William F. Buckley, Chuck donned a Red Army cap. With the photograph, Chuck sent a worn copy of Chairman Mao's **Little Red Book,** *which he found at a peddler's stall in the Moslem quarter of Xi'an. Buckley avowed himself inspired.*

The odd thing is, my wife is the most fiercely ethical person I know. She is also afraid of policemen. Driving alone one day, she noticed a police car behind her and slowed reflexively. She turned a corner and the black and white followed. In despair, she pulled carefully to the curb and waited. As the officer approached, she said, "Sir, please, what have I done?"

"You tell me, lady," he said. "You stopped."

Her explanation to me later was, like all women's explanations, supremely logical. "I *needed* those photographs," she said.

OCTOBER 24th Monday Day #6 USIA/CFA XI'AN

8:30 Tour Xi'an Studios, Run Red Sorghum

Our hosts in Xi'an rousted us out pretty early to see *Red Sorghum*, a highly touted Chinese film. We got there on time, the print of the film didn't, so they laid on an impromptu tour of the studio. Nothing is shooting there at the moment, so there wasn't much to see. I've seen an awful lot of sound stages and cutting rooms over the years. Never mind, we touched all the right bases. Eventually the print of *Red Sorghum* appeared and they ran it. It's very good, in fact, well worth waiting for. It's a story of Chinese resistance to the Japanese occupation as a background to some interesting social relationships. I think it would work well in international release, certainly at the film festivals, where foreign films always do well. **[This approval would of course not now be available to** *Red Sorghum,* **since Tiananmen Square. I've heard nothing of the film since I came home.]**

Barbara Zigli and Mme. Xie were determined to get us a meal in an honest-to-God Chinese restaurant (not segregated for tourists) and managed to find one for lunch. Unfortunately, the entire menu consisted of a variety of dumpling dishes, which I don't happen to like. They must've served twenty or more different kinds of dumplings, much enjoyed by Lydia and the other ladies. I did sketches and sipped on a Tsingtao beer.

Tonight, we were scheduled to screen a print of *El Cid* —imported by the USIA—for a select audience of Chinese filmmakers. We all arrived on time, only to find the projection room locked. The projectionist was on his dinner break.

We waited that out, then finally settled down to run the

film. The image flicked on, not to the opening credits, but to Reel 3. (Yes, you do come to know your films that well . . . the ones that play all the time, anyway.) I leapt up and raced for the projection booth, dragging Mme. Xie behind me. Of course, the projectionist had only a shaky knowledge of English numerals and had started off at random. I laid all the reels out in a row and Mme. Xie numbered them in Mandarin, accompanied by dire warnings. Back to our seats.

A good, clean print, displaying Bob Krasker's marvelous camera work, the striking credit designs, Miklos Rosas's marvelous score . . . then disaster again. The print was not subtitled in Mandarin, as promised; there was only the original English sound track. Happily, Mme. Xie was there beside me, as she has been almost from rising to bedtime since I set foot in China.

Once again, she saved the day. I muttered capsule comments as the story unfolded, which she then announced to the audience. "This is the Cid, a loyal knight . . . this is the woman who loves him . . . this is her father, who hates him . . . this is the king. These are the Moors; some of them are good, some are bad. These are the king's sons . . . this one is good . . . this other one is bad." Actually, the film worked very well with this kind of narrative. So it should. The best film scenes will work without any dialogue, which is close to what we had tonight. We also had a great success, which is always nice.

Of course, *El Cid* is a very Oriental story, dealing in honor and betrayal, love and hate, victory and death. That's why the film grossed so many millions in Japan. When I was in Kyoto for the opening there, a matriarch from a samurai family with no surviving males gave me a flawless samurai sword that had been in her family for seven hundred years. "You are a samurai," she said. What she really meant, of course, was that the Cid was a samurai. Exactly.

Well, it's a good film. It certainly proved itself tonight.

OCTOBER 25th Tuesday USIA Tour Day #7 XI'AN

My responsibilities were small today . . . a series of interviews at the hotel. That done, we visited a silk factory, with an opportunity to buy silk, a jade factory, also with opportunities in jade, and a painted panel factory, with etc., etc. Stumbling toward democracy, the Chinese have an advantage over the Soviets: They are instinctive capitalists, with experience stretching back a couple of millennia. In all its recorded history, Russia has known only an autocratic government.

We got back to the city in time to visit the Eighth Route Army Museum, a dusty compound where Mao Tse-tung and Chou En-lai sat during the early years of the war, waiting for the iron to grow hot enough to strike. I got the feeling, looking at all the photographs and artifacts, that Chou was the better man. Did they deify the wrong guy?

We had time, in the fading winter dusk, to walk on the old city wall. I've done this many times, in places all over the world where men first built walls to be safe from rape and pillage and the barbarous dark outside. Only weeks ago, we stood on the biggest: the Great Wall outside Beijing. Before that, the Pictish hill forts in pre-Roman Britain, Hadrian's Wall on the Scottish border, the medieval walls around the Spanish cities the Cid defended and assaulted, the Roman walls in Sagunto and North Africa, the Mayan walls in Cozumel, the Parthenon in Greece . . . all built, millennia past, to shield the fragile flower of civilization. I've never walked on one of them without getting some sense across the centuries of the men who watched there, sentinels, ". . . when earth's foundations trembled./ Who stood and took the sword stroke and are dead."

, there's only the obscene Berlin Wall, built
ns as a prison to keep people in, not out. I was
ate Department Representative to the Berlin Film
the summer of '61, the day they began it, when one
an tank could've ground it under. Ahh, but we never
t the tank. [Now the wall is gone, praise God . . . a generation late, but still a welcome consummation.]

We had dinner tonight in the hotel with Barbara Zigli
and Mme. Xie, both extraordinary women. Barbara seems to
me typical of the very best of the kind of young people the
Foreign Service is looking for. Intelligent, equipped, and
motivated . . . a younger version of Pat Corcoran, her boss.
We have lots of decent Americans . . . on farms and factories, in the military. It's just that the clowns and scumbags
get a lot of media space. Barbara's next posting is Taiwan.
They deserve her.

Mme. Xie is remarkable. The graceful dignity with
which she's survived her grossly demeaning experience in
the Cultural Revolution, including the death of her husband,
is testimony to the dimension of her spirit. We discussed a
horror story from that time about an accountant from the
People's Art Theatre where we mounted *Caine*. In balancing
his books, he noticed an error in the transfer of some funds
in U.S. dollars and crossed out a sum in the cents column. It
seems that the ideograph in written Mandarin for "cents" is
almost identical to the sign for "Mao." 毛 It was noted by
a diligent bureaucrat that this man had thus crossed out
Chairman Mao. So they killed him.

*In the elegant courtyard of the Great Mosque of Xi'an, Chuck
with Mme. Xie; Barbara Zigli of the USIA (now in Chengdu)
is in the foreground. Also fluent in Mandarin, Barbara helped
us through many a scrape and shared our last adventure, the
endless flight to Shanghai.*

*Mme. Xie, in fine form atop the huge wall of Xi'an. What a
truly great woman she is!*

OCTOBER 26th Wednesday USIA Tour Day #8

Fly to SHANGHAI

Traveling for pleasure . . . and this end of the trip is partly that . . . only began something over a century ago. Before then, there were no tourists. You only left home if the Vandals showed up on the hills or Viking longships grounded on the beach, intent on rape and pillage. There were, of course, those itchy wanderers intent on discovering the New World, or conquering France, as well as a few sports like Herodotus and Gibbon . . . and Marco Polo. Other than that, people largely stayed home.

By the mid-1900s, though, Englishmen who could afford it, along with a few Americans, were undertaking the "Grand Tour," sketchbook in hand, to record the Pyramids, the Roman Forum, and the Grand Canal. Tourists planned for luxury, but often put up with slum conditions. Now, of course, the planet spins under our feet, so restless are we for far places.

God knows, I've done more than my share of travel, almost all of it in pursuit of my living or attending the wars they asked me to go to. Over the years, I've endured the usual traveler's troubles: the Odyssey of the Lost Luggage, or, "I went to Indianapolis, but my bag got to go to Istanbul"; the Diarrhea Decathlon for most days spent flat on your back in a far place. A major category is air travel. Today, we earned a Personal Worst there.

It seemed like a piece of cake. A noon departure, which meant we could sleep in a bit (I'm still winding down from the *Caine* schedule), easy packing time, an hour and a half to

Shanghai, where a full schedule of interviews and seminars waited, but no more than a good day's work.

Mme. Xie and Barbara Z. were skeptical. (Good name for a travel agency there: "Xie & Z. The World at Your Feet.") "Let's go out a little early . . . you never know when there'll be complications," they said.

"Couldn't we just phone?" No, not a wise idea. So we left early for the airport in our blue van full of bags and us in ample anticipation of unstated contingencies.

Xi'an's airport is small, with a modest parking lot. "You guys wait here in the van; we'll check things out," Barbara said. She didn't say "check you in," I noted, so she was reconnoitering. Not a good sign. She was back in twenty minutes. "The flight for Shanghai is three hours late."

"OK," I said, ever the philosopher. "That gives us time to go back into town and have a good lunch." No-o-o . . . not possible. The plane might in fact come in at any time. We must be ready. "Well, let's get a bite in the airport tea shop." There wasn't one, nor even any vending machines. In an hour, Barbara came back with a Butterfinger bar and a warm beer. God knows where she stole them . . . and He will surely forgive her. Lydia and I shared the bar, the beer, and the thin comfort that we had plenty to read.

By midafternoon, toilets became a priority. I made do with a bush by the fence, but Lydia, suffering yet another example of God's discrimination against women, had to find facilities inside the terminal. She came back relieved, but resentful. "I've never seen a worse john," she said. "There's not only no paper, there's no sign there ever *was* any. And the smell would choke a hyena."

Meantime, our resourceful Xie & Z. team were hard at work inside, though the odds were mounting. The plane we were waiting for, it became clear, was not today's flight to Shanghai, but yesterday's. There was a full complement of passengers already encamped to board it. What's more, there were people in the terminal who'd been waiting there for two days. Well, defeat, then. Mmm . . . not necessarily. Oriental guile and diplomatic wile were busy.

At 4:00 PM, Barbara Z. came to the van, triumphantly waving four boarding passes. "We can check in the luggage," she said. Much to and fro with porters, careful segregation of the checked bags from the carry-ons. High spirits all around, until it became clear that there were somehow eight bags, not all of them small, unchecked. I was the only male in a party of four; clearly I was responsible for hand-carrying almost all of that. It was doable, but only in two trips, with Xie, Z., or Lydia at either end.

First, let's find a VIP lounge, for however long we still have to wait. No, there *is* no VIP (obviously untrue . . . in a Communist country particularly, there will be a VIP). We stand in a hallway for half an hour, till Lydia, on another trip to the fetid Ladies' Room, notes an unmistakable VIP lounge, behind discreet lace curtains. Xie & Z. lunge into action, to no avail. This lounge is only for Very Important People (obviously thin on the ground, since it's locked and dark). Xie & Z. point out that we have here not only VIPs, but IIPs (Incredibly Important People), doing a vast service to the People's Republic of China and in desperate need of a place to sit down. No dice.

After half an hour of standing in a corner, huddled around our eight carry-ons, I went to the men's room (better the bush in the parking lot). I noticed light and movement in the forbidden VIP and an unlocked door. We made a dash for it (two trips for me with the carry-ons). Inside was an affable pair of certifiable Chinese VIPs. A less affable bureaucrat appeared, outraged at our trespass, but we overrode him and collapsed into real chairs. There were also ample Cokes (though warm) behind the bar. Also crackers.

At 10:00 PM, we were summoned to the boarding gate, still lacking any information whatever on when the plane might land, or whether we could board it, passes regardless.

Freedom of information does not have a high priority in the various people's republics. Another desperate, two-lap dash with the carry-ons. Worse, my welcome anonymity in China was snatched away. Waiting in the boarding area was a group of Germans and another of Chinese-Americans. All were delighted to recognize me, all eager with autograph books, Instamatics, and videocams. It was a difficult hour.

In the end, we stumbled on board another bloody Ilyushin, clutching our bloody carry-ons, and arrived in Shanghai at 1:00 AM, my work schedule scrubbed, but blissfully happy to settle into an extraordinary suite at the Sheraton Hua Ting. We collapsed into a bed at least eight feet square, where I tossed and turned for all of twenty seconds.

OCTOBER 27th Thursday USIA Tour Day #9 Shanghai

I don't think I've ever slept in such a big bed. Catherine the Great could easily have handled three imperial guardsmen in it. I woke disoriented, aware only of a vast stretch of mattress beneath me. As sometimes happens (to me, anyway), when I'm overtraveled and underslept, I couldn't remember where I was. This needs careful handling. You don't want to move, or open more than one eye, till you've figured out where the hell you are, so you can deal with whatever it is. (Be there monsters?)

Where *is* this? Not London . . . no. No, not home, dummy . . . you *know* that! Not even the U.S. It's amazing how hard it can be to jump-start your brain out of sleep. In the end, I got it, noted my girl sleeping deeply several feet away in the far reaches of the bed and slid out to pad naked, exploring. (Ah, there's a breathless tidbit for the public. I never wear pajamas, even in the movies.)

This suite is far larger and grander than I realized last night. I've been in some in Las Vegas almost as big, but repulsively glitzy . . . you can't sleep for the sequins reflecting in the mirrors over the bed. These rooms are all superb examples of Chinese design. To my eye, a lot of the pieces look genuine.

There are three bedrooms on the second floor, all large, with exotically Jacuzzied bathrooms. Downstairs are tiled halls, a study, a vast sitting room, a dining room with a kitchen and a table that could seat twenty. As the thin, predawn loom brightened toward morning, I climbed to the roof terrace (large enough to land a chopper) and leaned on the railing, watching the day break over Shanghai, thirty stories below. Well, I thought, feeling the sun warm on my shoulders . . . I spent three days in a tent, shooting on top of Mount Sinai . . . it all balances out.

An hour later, I was showered, dressed, breakfasted, and into my interviews. When Lydia's breakfast came, she got lost trying to find the dining room. "How can they possibly afford to give us this suite?" she said.

"Darling," I said, "a suite like this is given more often than it's rented. This wasn't built for the likes of us. Heads of state are seldom charged to visit a country. Just be sure not to break anything."

The late plane yesterday ruined our schedule; we couldn't reset the screening/seminar we blew for this afternoon. That gave us time, when I'd finished my press stuff, to tour the riverfront, in British times among the important ports in the world, and the Bund, once ranked as a major financial center. We also walked in the park along the river where the People's Republic has cannily preserved the old sign, in English: NO DOGS OR CHINESE. I had a nice time doing nothing and Lydia worked out her cameras well.

Tonight was the last of our time in China. We spent it in the sybaritic indulgence of our suite, high above this ancient city and the spin it's given and has yet to give to history. It was a fine way to end. I hope I earned it.

[The next day, we flew home, in a 747 that took off and landed on schedule. Showing my passport to the Immigration officer, I felt the pleasure I always do at his "Welcome home." I wonder if those guys know how good that is to hear? I also felt very good about the *Caine*'s voyage to China. I never in God's world would've thought of it by myself, but it was truly an offer I couldn't refuse. The idea of doing that play in China with a Chinese cast was so formidable a challenge that I never could've looked at myself shaving if I'd ducked it. ("What about that play you were going to direct in Beijing, Chuck . . . in *Chinese,* was it?" "Oh, I passed on that, finally. This interesting film came up at Fox . . .") No, you have to do it.

I remember when Frank Schaffner and I were asked to do *Macbeth* in the Paleolithic Age of live TV. "Absolutely!" we said. Could you cut it to ninety minutes? "Why not?" Ten days rehearsal enough? "I guess so. I played it before, in college." Of course, we were only twenty-six, when you don't *know* anything, but you're positive you can *do* anything. Never mind. The point is, there are moments in your life you can't let go by.

My whole life was shaped by one of them. When Lydia and I were at Northwestern before I left for WW II, still unattached, but in love (me at least), she told me she was going out to dinner with a high school boyfriend and half a dozen other people. I accepted this, grudgingly, but on that night, I went to the restaurant with a prepared speech, which evaporated as I walked in the door. I stood there a moment trying to remember my lines, then took her by the hand and said, "You have to come with me."

She did, too. We were married before I went overseas. Aside from surviving the war, which I didn't have a lot to do with, this was the most significant action of my life.

You can see why I believe in seizing the moment. Even

In Shanghai on our last day we lunched at what would correspond to the Screen Actors Guild in the U.S. Again, the actors seemed entirely familiar, artists-of-the-blood. The lovely Chinese actress with Chuck is among their most prominent and successful performers. We left China the next day, feeling that we had seen a great deal of that vast country, but hoping to go back another time to see more of the countryside and the people. Strange, beautiful, ancient China! Marco Polo, where are you now?

if *Caine* had been a disaster, it would've been worth trying. In the event, it turned out. We learned a great deal . . . not only about directing, for me, but about China. I could've toured the country for six months and learned less about it than I did in two, working there.

The play ran all through the winter. They took it up for a successful engagement in Shanghai, then brought it back to the PAT, where it was still running in early June, when the demonstrations began in Tiananmen Square. I learned a while ago that our actors gathered there, wearing the jackets I gave them with the *Caine* logo on the back and carrying a sign that said *The Caine Mutiny Court-martial*. That evening, the power was cut at the theatre, making it impossible to perform. Since then, I've gotten a letter from my stage manager, now in Singapore, translated into very guarded English. My contacts in the State Department advise against trying to reach any of the Chinese I worked with, for fear it would worsen their situation. I'm still glad I did the play. I'll bet they are, too.]